Jesus Christ Mystery Teachings Through Parables

Recognize Amazing Lifeforce Energy Within Yourself

Articles come from the "King James Bible."
(The Gospels According to Matthew)

Dedication

This book is dedicated to all souls for Love to enter into their domain.

Acknowledgment

I want to thank my Lord and Savior, Jesus Christ, for His Love and enduring patience leading to my righteous thinking and enlightenment.

Prelude

The New Testament used for this booklet comes from the King James version.

Matthew, **Mark**, **Luke**, and **John** give excellent insights into the most extraordinary human being who ever lived here on this planet in the four books.

Who is Jesus Christ?

Matthew 11:9

Jesus Christ, Lord God, the Messiah, accounted for many eyewitness miracles on record.

In this state of consciousness, the "First Begotten" had become fully adaptable far beyond the 5th Dimension.

We, (you and I) are presently living on a 3rd Dimensional planet; we are here in the physical to unfold our spiritual knowledge and growth into light beings.

For Jesus Christ, "God" manifested in the flesh, did indeed perform several miracles, and wonders no other earthly being has ever done.

Let the reader understand and consider Jesus spoke in parables (spiritual truths) for God's chosen elect seeking facts into God's will, which is Love and Truth.

In other words, while you are gaining spiritual insights and expanding your conscious awareness, take a moment to open your mind's eye of Love into these teachings.

You will unlock your unlimited potential by exploring **Universal Laws** at play in every moment of your life! Make no mistake, **Jesus is Lord God** in trinity!

God the Father, God the Son, and God the Holy Spirit.

Author's Note

These testimonies will expand your conscious awareness of truths.

You will discover why this booklet will set you *free*! The actual value is spiritual worth, regardless of if you are male, female, *Christian*, *Buddhism*, *Muslim*, black, white, Asian, or even Jewish.

The truth will expand your Love to all! This booklet will develop and answer all that there is to life.

We all have come to search or seek out why we are here on earth? In addition to the question, what is my purpose for being here?

This book is worth more than any price of gold or silver than you can ever imagine. Likewise, as you read scriptures, let me encourage you to allow our Lord Jesus Christ into your light.

Therefore, his guidance can bring about more clarity and understanding to *his will*, Love, and truth.

To add value to your time, please feel free to use the *Glossary Index* portion in this booklet to assist you in any way you sense is appropriate.

Consequently, you will find yourself listening with more intent on finding righteous thoughts leading you to the kingdom of *God*.

You will sleep with this booklet as you rejoice with the Son of Man in his glory. As you read scripture in mind, one can indeed hear our Lord Jesus's voice (Listen with intent).

Brother, sister, please allow me to open my Love and light to the very thing you are seeking. Jesus Christ, Lord and Savior, God in Trinity here and right now!

May God continue to bless you on your soul's journey to a path of righteousness leading to enlightenment.

Table of Contents

Matthew Chapter 3 1

Matthew Chapter 4 4

Matthew Chapter 5 10

Matthew Chapter 6 48

Matthew Chapter 7 70

Matthew Chapter 8 86

Matthew Chapter 9 93

Matthew Chapter 10 102

Matthew Chapter 11 122

Matthew Chapter 12 135

Matthew Chapter 13 154

Matthew Chapter 14 180

Matthew Chapter 15 182

Matthew Chapter 16 192

Matthew Chapter 17 202

Matthew Chapter 18 209

Matthew Chapter 19 228

Matthew Chapter 20 238

Matthew Chapter 21 252

Matthew Chapter 22 266

Matthew Chapter 23 279

Matthew Chapter 24 298

Matthew Chapter 25 320

Matthew Chapter 26 341

Matthew Chapter 27 355

Matthew Chapter 28 356

INDEX 359

Matthew Chapter 3

KJV Matthew 3: verse 15

And Jesus answering said unto him, Suffer *it to be so* now: for thus it becometh us to fulfill all righteousness. Then he suffered unto him.

Comment appropriately to "Suffer *it to be so* now."

Immediately, we begin with our first parable, this opens God's New Commandments in the New Testament.

For Jesus is the Christ, the Messiah, Son of God, and Savior of all humanity to suffer does not mean he was inflicted with pain physically or spiritually.

In this case, *"to suffer"* means surrendering to a higher purpose given through the Holy Spirit by our Heavenly Father.

Jesus Christ humbled himself by allowing John the Baptist to baptize him. Later, we will discover the importance of enabling spiritual guidance for every soul's journey to enlightenment.

We all will eventually get there!

Additionally, the prophet Daniel foretold the coming of the Lord to end all suffering.

In these parables you are holding ends this anguish once and for all. "You now have the answers to your purpose."

Comment appropriately to "for thus it becometh us to fulfill all righteousness."

"Up until this moment of John Baptizing Christ, the completion of the baptism was with water. The Messiah, Jesus Christ, is anointed to baptize you with the Holy Spirit (Righteous thinking).

In this act of pure Love in giving of one's life on the cross, essentially allowing the closing of God's Laws given unto Moses. As a result, this opens the way of accepting the teachings of Jesus Christ given in the New Testament.

Consequently, we can show later in scripture what Jesus says concerning the Old Testament. In conclusion, it is formerly known as the First Testament.

Jesus said, "Think not that I am come to destroy the law or the prophets: I am not come to destroy, but to fulfill."

Matthew 5: 17

In other words, to fulfill anything is to bring closure to it! In addition, the Old Testament or the law of Moses concluded with, "*It is finished.*" Our Lord's completion of work given unto him from the Father.

John 19: 30

<u>Indeed, this brings the New Testament ways to enter God's Kingdom to the forefront.</u>

Besides, our Lord and Savior knew the Old Testament was perplexing by the religious leader's many edits and because of this.

Many revisions led to denominations of influence; divisions of churches began adding earthly riches of men followed by power not given from heaven.

Matthew Chapter 4

KJV Matthew 4: Verse 4

But he answered and said, It is written, Man shall not live by bread alone, but by every word that proceedeth out of the mouth of God.

Comment appropriately to "It is written, Man shall not live by bread alone."

In this parable, bread or leaven is an expression of spiritual guidance. When reciting the Lord's prayer, we say, *"Give us this day, our daily bread."*

In receiving daily bread, we turn our conscious thoughts to biblical or spiritual guidance in all forms.

We have set our intentions to allow for spiritual growth in our reading the bible, transcendental meditation, listening to uplifting music, or other forms of Godliness.

Comment appropriately to "but by every word that proceedeth out of the mouth of God."

How do we receive every word by the mouth of God?

To receive every word by the mouth of God is done by ***transcendental meditation (TM)***.

We must discipline ourselves and learn how to *"be still" before God with intentions* for a bit of time and remove all forms of distractions from our lives.

(*These are the actual hidden teachings within the parables of Jesus Christ*).

Likewise, together, we will explore consciousness in the unity of oneness. So, let's continue, shall we?

KJV Matthew 4: Verse 7

Jesus said unto him, It is written again, Thou shalt not tempt the Lord thy God.

Comment appropriately to "It is written again."

Jesus is affirming to those teaching from the Old Testament Law of Moses. My New Commandments are from the Father in the New Testament and are living.

Before we move forward, let's discern the term "Living" Jesus Christ, and what it means? The term "Living Jesus Christ" indicates that he was of full consciousness and anointed by the Holy Spirit. And for this reason, the New Testament becomes a living consciousness of truths and serves now as the Word of God.

Note: Thus, this brings closure to the Old Testament, formerly known as the First Testament of the bible, upon crucifixion.

Comment appropriately to "Thou shalt not tempt the Lord thy God."

Do not tempt your Lord God within your heart, soul, and mind. For the unseen Father in Heaven Loves you and sees all things. He dwells within us and outside of us. Therefore, he knows all things, our every thought, intent, and desire.

So, to challenge his Love, power, goodness, and mercy falls under the "*Universal Law Cause and Effect*." Therefore, your inequity thoughts and intent will manifest in darkness.

KJV Matthew 4: Verse 10

Then saith Jesus unto him, Get thee hence, Satan: for it is written, Thou shalt worship the Lord thy God, and him only shalt thou serve.

Comment appropriately to "Get thee hence, Satan."

In other words, "Farewell Satan." Jesus fasted for forty days in the wilderness to prepare himself for his ministry. He began by cleansing his spirit of all worldly thoughts or material desires.

To fast is what our Heavenly Father intended us to do often, and that is, take a break from worldly attachments.

Likewise, when we fast in the human body, we do not gain any spiritual insights. Indeed, we create a vibrational misalignment causing stress to ourselves, harming our souls from an abundance of Love within consciousness.

For this reason, a spiritual fast (*transcendental meditation),* we must learn to evaluate our dependency on worldly attachments such as our handheld devices, computers, or things that we cannot take with us into the afterlife.

There is no devil. Satan doesn't even exist in a spiritual form!

Instead, Satan is used throughout the bible as a metaphor to characterize man's mind. Basically, to be or state of mind, hence spiritually dead.

For there is *God* and *man, and therefore,* ***God*** is of perfect consciousness. Thus, ***man*** is the substance of the human mind portraying both good and evil.

Comment appropriately to "for it is written, Thou shalt worship the Lord thy God, and him only shalt thou serve."

In God's new commandment, Jesus is stating we are of one consciousness and to serve in him is to help them *all*.

KJV Matthew 4: Verse 17

From that time, Jesus began to preach, and to say, Repent: for the kingdom of heaven is at hand.

Comment appropriately to "Repent:"

Confess your sins; do not hide them within your heart because the Father sees all things.

Comment appropriately to "for the kingdom of heaven is at hand."

The kingdom of heaven is a full conscious awakening to unconditional Love in the heart. (God's will).

The pathway to unconditional Love is through Christ Jesus. Our Lord stated, *"I am the way, the truth, and the life."*

KJV Matthew 4: Verse 19

And he saith unto them, Follow me, and I will make you fishers of men.

Comment appropriately to "Follow me,"

"Follow me" is what Christ intended it to mean. Do not deviate from his teachings of righteous thinking.

Comment appropriately to "and I will make you fishers of men."

The teachings of Jesus Christ will lead you to his will, which is the same of our Heavenly Father's will of unconditional Love.

Once you have become fully awakened into Self-realization, "*fishers of men.*"

Other souls may experience an ah feeling in your presence and can sense their emotions with the fully awakened Chosen elect. Many will be incapable of expressing how or what they are feeling concerning the soul with full consciousness.

Nonetheless, allow others in your presence to accept your light in your vibrations. Bring healing from words of Love.

Matthew Chapter 5

KJV Matthew 5: Verse 3

"**B**lessed *are* the poor in spirit: for theirs is the kingdom of heaven."

Comment appropriately to "Blessed *are* the poor in spirit:"

Remember, Jesus' teachings are spiritual. Not of this physical earthly plane!

Blessed is those who become insufficient in the subconscious mind, free from worldly attachments. To obtain or have no worldly passions leading to attachments.

Before we move forward, let's find purpose in this verse because this doesn't necessarily mean you can't have the latest whatever in life!

Nonetheless, the renewing of the mind in conscious thought must become a way of being. Thus, your dependency on worldly connections to material desires. In this case, we refer to things outside of the mind that we cannot take upon physical death.

Comment appropriately to "for theirs is the kingdom of heaven."

For the elect, the kingdom of heaven is conscious awareness. In other words, you become the purity of thoughts in the mind. Thus, you give pure light to all!

KJV Matthew 5: Verse 4

"Blessed *are* they that mourn: for they shall be comforted."

Comment appropriately to "Blessed *are* they that mourn:"

Blessed is those sure to endure a paradigm shift of consciousness in their awakening.

Comment appropriately to "for they shall be comforted."

To be comforted is to find peace within the subconscious mind. Therefore, we find that the Holy Spirit of the Father rests within us when praying or during transcendental meditation.

Over time and through stillness, a child of God can obtain an awakening and be freed through the Holy Spirit. Thus, *"Whom the Son sets free is free indeed."*

Note: No one said finding the Kingdom of God was going to be easy; you must do the shadow work our Father has given you to do.

You must make a conscious effort to seek truths that lie within your true nature. But, more importantly, this brings more focus to the interpretation of "*know thyself.*"

KJV Matthew 5: Verse 5

"Blessed *are* the meek: for they shall inherit the earth."

Comment appropriately to "Blessed *are* the meek"

Blessed is those who obtain conscious thoughts of Love through awareness.

Comment appropriately to "for they shall inherit the earth."

In seeking God's Kingdom, inheriting the earth, your inner world is likened to inheriting your subconscious mind and giving it inner peace. Its natural state of being!

Note: "To inherit the earth, small "e" does *not* refer to "Gaia, Mother Earth." Later, we will explore in the Lord's prayer where is states; "in earth, as it is in heaven." *Matthew 6:10*

KJV Matthew 5: Verse 6

"Blessed *are* they which do hunger and thirst after righteousness: for they shall be filled."

Comment appropriately to "Blessed *are* they which do hunger and thirst after righteousness:"

Blessed is those who desire spiritual truths; to hunger is to seek spiritual food for the soul. It expands conscious awareness through the teachings of Jesus Christ.

Spiritual food for the spiritual body can come from many sources.

However, the fruit tree that bears good fruit gives righteous thinking through awareness; furthermore, it advances the purity of knowledge and understanding necessary for enlightenment.

Remember, you must intend to "be still" for a while to hear by the "mouth of God." (*Matthew 4; 4*).

Water or to thirst refers to the substance of the mind for one who is seeking good thoughts for clarity; hence, wisdom from the conscious recognition of oneness.

Comment appropriately to "for they shall be filled."

For those chosen ones will be filled with light, conscious awareness of all truths —no hidden secrets.

KJV Matthew 5: Verse 7

"Blessed *are* the merciful: for they shall obtain mercy."

Comment appropriately to "Blessed *are* the merciful:"

Blessed is those who find peacefulness in the subconscious mind.

Note: When mercy is necessary, conscious awareness bears the action of forgiveness to all children of God. In essence, we must allow for forgiveness in all situations and circumstances.

Comment appropriately to "for they shall obtain mercy."

For those called to righteousness will find peace in the

subconscious mind.

Note: In all cases, to give or receive mercy is to find love and peace.

KJV Matthew 5: Verse 8

Blessed *are* the pure in heart: for they shall see God."

Comment appropriately to "Blessed *are* the pure in heart:"

Blessed are those aligned in conscious thought—purity of the subconscious mind leads to purity of heart. Aligning the core to our senses and emotions plays a vital role in the subconscious mind.

Once you are consciously aware of your feelings, healing and forgiveness become a state of being relatively quickly.

In other words, for this "B" attitude, this "state of being" begins with the purity of the mind leading to the heart.

One can become non-judging of all things. For this reason, we must remove our thoughts from judgment in all states of the mind. For instance, voting elections, they too are a form of judging.

When we remove judging in thought, the mind finds peace within the workings of the subconscious mind. Free to allow for Love in harmonious relationships.

One can become forgiving of everyone and everything. But, without forgiveness, this can lead to anger which is no doubt inward pain.

One is in alignment with conscious awareness.

Note: Accept this truth within your heart, there is no such thing as right or wrong, for there is only **Love**. Each of us view things from our perspective.

Purity within the mind leads to purity of heart—a state of being.

Comment appropriately to "for they shall see God."

The appointed elected soul will experience a shared likeness of the Father and shared power from within their domain.

KJV Matthew 5: Verse 9

Blessed *are* the peacemakers: for they shall be called the children of God.

Comment appropriately to "Blessed *are* the peacemakers:"

Blessed is those who subdue their divided subconscious human-mind, for they shall find a reconciliation of righteous thoughts. In essence, Angelic thoughts come from the heart by way of God's Kingdom or the King's domain.

We are here on a soul's journey to experience Love, and in this purpose, our Heavenly Fathers' will be done. Sometimes, we can feel alone because of our alter ego-mind (human-mind) resting in our nature subconsciously. This idea of separation from God stems from a subtle low vibration in misalignment.

Realizing our true nature takes effort on a souls' behalf. Take comfort in knowing you are from the Kingdom of Heaven, and upon physical death, you shall return!

Comment appropriately to "for they shall be called the children of God."

Once you can subdue the human subconscious mind, eternal peace rests within conscious awareness.

Hence, you become one with God as a child, full of happiness, free in mind and from bondage.

Note: When the Holy Spirit has anointed the Chosen elect. Likewise, in renewing the mind their state of mind is peaceful.

KJV Matthew 5: Verse 10

Blessed *are* they which are persecuted for righteousness sake: for theirs is the kingdom of heaven."

Comment appropriately to "Blessed *are* they which are persecuted for righteousness sake:"

They, the elect, are being anointed by the Holy Spirit in the renewing of the mind.

The subconscious mind may feel tormented by a little suffering, which is inevitable. Nonetheless, Love carries you from one location to the next.

Gaining insights and truths during a spiritual awakening can be overwhelming at times. However, expanding the mind brings about understanding, goodness, and a soul's oneness through Jesus Christ.

Comment appropriately to "for theirs is the kingdom of heaven."

The kingdom of heaven refers to the conscious mind given to each soul upon their journey. Thus, we always have a piece of home with us.

Close your eyes; you can experience home at this very moment! The reality of both the spiritual and material substance of matter (an energy element of nothingness) form an eternal, indestructible, boundless, and infinite energy field.

Conversely, you are from it, and you are part of it.

KJV Matthew 5: Verse 11

Blessed are ye, when *men* shall revile you, and persecute *you*, and shall say all manner of evil against you falsely, for my sake."

Comment appropriately to "Blessed are ye, when *men* shall revile you,"

You beautify the mind through the teachings of Jesus Christ. There will be religious leaders and teachers of the law who will criticize and denounce this way of worship.

In other words, be grateful because you have placed peace within your subconscious mind. But unfortunately, religious teachers have no way of finding this peace with their alter ego-mind (human-mind).

Through meditation with intentions, you create an admission into the teachings of Jesus Christ by way of our Heavenly Father. **These are the works given unto each soul necessary for Self-realization.**

Special Note: Be aware that most souls are misaligned and may dislike you for your state of being, which is peace. This inner anger may reflect their souls inner work necessary to obtain peace of mind. Remain at peace, this subtle vibration can in some cases be felt.

In most cases, when a soul has not achieved this level of understanding, one can feel the *Universal Law of Polarity* within their spiritual body.

Comment appropriately to "and persecute you,"

Religious teachers and others who are spiritually sleeping may become outraged and even expel you from their sight. In addition, they fail themselves by not allowing a way for the gospels of Love and truth to be revealed. Christ said:

Let them alone: they be blind leaders of the blind. And if the blind lead the blind, both shall fall into the ditch.

(Matthew 15:14)

Note: Blind leaders are teachers of the law of Moses (Old Testament).

Comment appropriately to and shall say all manner of evil against you falsely, for my sake."

At any rate, religious and blind leaders sneeringly objected against the teachings of Jesus Christ, for there were prophets who were mistreated in the same manner for the sake of Love and truth.

KJV Matthew 5: Verse 12

Rejoice, and be exceeding glad: for great is your reward in heaven: for so persecuted they the prophets which were before you."

Comment appropriately to "Rejoice, and be exceeding glad:"

Delight yourself in the renewing of the subconscious mind.

Comment appropriately to "for great is your reward in heaven:"

Because you accepted the teachings of Jesus Christ, enormous works can transcend the consciousness of the Self.

Note: To make this easier for you; your **conscious mind** (heaven) is a shared mind with **all** from your Higher Self (God) which provides purity of thoughts and desires.

Your **subconscious mind** is **yours** and is considered your inner world, which holds your emotions and feelings; and not to mention it stores all your life's memories.

Your **super-conscious mind** is located near your heart. It is centralized within your heart center chakra; it allows for pure navigation in life. If you can accept this truth, your heart can never steer you away from the truth. It is a choice you get to make in each moment, because of your "free will".

Lastly, the **alter ego-mind** (human mind) is the mind that sees what is before you in false realities. (Both Good and Evil).

Comment appropriately to "for so persecuted they the prophets which were before you."

All who have come before us may have felt these types of afflictions possible during a spiritual awakening.

When a mind is divided in the alter ego away from truths. It cannot weigh against realities and evil. Thus, it is against itself, leaving a reason to believe it is the body, which means in mind, no peace.

Note: Because of this, persecution for righteous thought ensues the renewing of the mind. Thus, the alter ego or the "I" in I am creates feelings of separation from oneness with God.

KJV Matthew 5: Verse 13

Ye are the salt of the earth: but if the salt have lost his savour, wherewith shall it be salted? It is thenceforth good for nothing, but to be cast out, and to be trodden under foot of men.

Comment appropriately to "Ye are the salt of the earth: but if the salt have lost his savour, wherewith shall it be salted?"

For starters, salt refers to a substance of the mind in your ocean, meaning it is also a substance of emotions in mind. Thus, you are the feelings and emotions in the subconscious mind. **(Ye are the salt).**

Earth, small "e" relates to the subconscious mind. But be that as it may, salt is not its entirety of consciousness.

Emotions derive through thoughts and desires from the conscious mind; consequently, you do not take responsibility for righteous thinking **(lost savor)**. You deny or omit the divine purity of feelings and emotions over your subconscious mind.

How will you escape living within a divided mind of discord? Not to mention, you remain spiritually dead **(wherewith shall it be salted).**

Comment appropriately to "it is thenceforth good for nothing, but to be cast out, and to be trodden under foot of men."

Without obtaining consciousness of the Self, you are without light for others to follow.

Yet, at the same time, we accept the altered ego state of mind by believing we are the human mind (good for nothing). Hence, a divided mind leading to both good and evil.

Wherefore, we portray evil thoughts followed by evil deeds (be cast out).

In this case, to become trodden is to become stepped on for

your lack of moral or spiritual values in society.

KJV Matthew 5: Verse 14

Ye are the light of the world. A city that is set on an hill cannot be hid.

Comment appropriately to "Ye are the light of the world.

Ye or you refer to those who are consciously aware of the workings within your subconscious mind (light of the world).

Comment appropriately to "A city that is set on an hill cannot be hid."

The fully awakened soul cannot withhold the teachings (cannot be hid) from those searching for truths.

KJV Matthew 5: Verse 15

Neither do men light a candle, and put it under a bushel, but on a candlestick; and it giveth light unto all that are in the house.

Comment appropriately to "Neither do men light a candle, and put it under a bushel, but on a candlestick;"

Surrounding this parable, men are not pursuing righteous thought (men do not light a candle) by remaining in darkness. On the contrary, they stay in ignorance of truths (put it under a bushel). However, when you come to dwell in the light.

Comment appropriately to "and it giveth light unto all that are in the house."

This light will give the conscious and subconscious mind truths in full awareness of the soul (house).

KJV Matthew 5: Verse 16

Let your light so shine before men, that they may see your good works, and glorify your Father which is in heaven.

Comment appropriately to "Let your light so shine before men,"

Upon completing spiritual awakening (shine your light before men), you become consciously aware of the Self. Thus, you become light for all to follow.

Comment appropriately to "that they may see your good works, and glorify your Father which is in heaven."

These works in solitude (your good works) will reveal Jesus' will, which is inner peace through harmonious relationships. So, to be state of mind, full of Love and truths in conscious awareness.

KJV Matthew 5: Verse 17

Think not that I am come to destroy the law, or the prophets: I am not come to destroy, but to fulfil.

Comment appropriately to "Think not that I am come to destroy the law, or the prophets":

In this parable, we find how the Messiah is bringing forth Love and guidance to the Kingdom of God. In the law, "I," the alter ego in "I am," denounced the Word of God's way of being.

Teachers of the law (prophets) hid truths on entering God's kingdom with edits leading to denominations.

Comment appropriately to "I am not come to destroy, but to fulfill"

For with my New Commandment, surely, I will bring completion (fulfill) to the Old Testament Law of Moses.

KJV Matthew 5: Verse 18

For verily I say unto you, Till heaven and earth pass, one jot or one tittle shall in no wise pass from the law, till all be fulfilled.

Comment appropriately to "For verily I say unto you,"

Take notice to the elect; he passes on his ministry's truths or how to proceed to righteousness. "Verily I say unto you," which serves as an alert notification to the electors of the teachers of the new commandments.

Comment appropriately to "Till heaven and earth pass,"

Jesus Christ is announcing his death on the cross of the human body. Heaven spelled with a small "h" and earth small "e" refers to the inner workings of his own conscious and subconscious mind.

Notice that Jesus is also referring to the inner workings of the mind. For this (heaven; conscious mind) and (earth;

subconscious mind) reveal truths of the alter ego-mind. (Human mind)

Living in a divided mind leads to the torment of the mind accessing both good and evil. So then, upon physical death, these minds pass away, leaving the soul to share the mind of God eternal.

Comment appropriately to "one jot or one tittle shall in no wise pass from the law."

In the Old Testament of the bible, formerly known as the "First Testament." All laws given unto Moses will not become abolished because grace shows no abound (one jot or tittle shall not pass away).

In truth, Jesus is referring to the New Testament and the new teachings from our Heavenly Father. These laws were to remain in place until his crucifixion.

Comment appropriately to "till all be fulfilled."

To fulfill anything is to bring completion or closure. In this case, the prophets foretold of a Messiah to come into the world and end all suffering. Also, notice all in this context to mean all souls. Thus, "all be fulfilled".

"We all will eventually get there to enlightenment!"

The Living Jesus Christ fulfillment by crucifixion completes not only ending the Old Testament. It brings about a renewing of mind with baptism by the Holy Spirit.

KJV Matthew 5: Verse 19

Whosoever therefore shall break one of these least commandments, and shall teach men so, he shall be called the least in the kingdom of heaven: but whosoever shall do and teach *them*, the same shall be called great in the kingdom of heaven.

Comment appropriately to "Whosoever therefore shall break one of these least commandments, and shall teach men so,"

This parable refers to religious leaders or those with groups of followers. Jesus is referring to the New Testament, which holds his new commandments of Love and truth.

To direct audiences, groups, or followers away from the "New Testament" is misguiding souls. Christ said:

And he spake a parable unto them, Can the blind lead the blind? Shall they not both fall into the ditch?

Luke 6:39

To govern men, men refer to the physical being looking for direction. These leaders must do so by remaining in the teachings found in the New Testament, not the Old Testament.

Comment appropriately to "he shall be called the least in the kingdom of heaven:"

To advise or guide his sheep outside of the new commandments or teachings. He shall lose favor in spiritual abundance. His conscious awareness will be filled with darkness.

Comment appropriately to "but whosoever shall do and teach *them*, the same shall be called great in the kingdom of heaven."

Advisers who do good deeds and revel in the "Teachings of Christ" shall manifest more conscious awareness.

KJV Matthew 5: Verse 20

For I say unto you, That except your righteousness shall exceed *the righteousness* of the scribes and Pharisees, ye shall in no case enter into the kingdom of heaven.

Comment appropriately to "For I say unto you, That except your righteousness shall exceed *the righteousness* of the scribes and Pharisees,"

Our Lord God gives light to this parable, to alert his disciples of knowing why his teachings are the new commandments. He explains why to not deviate from his teachings which give purity of mind leading to righteous thoughts.

Thus, to veer away from his New Testament teachings, you shall remain in darkness as the scribes and Pharisees, incapable of sharing light.

Comment appropriately to "ye shall in no case enter into the kingdom of heaven."

In your disobedience of "not" following the new

commandments, you will in no way unfold and discover the five trees in Paradise which remain undisturbed and whose leaves do not fall.

Note: The five trees that remain undisturbed in Paradise would happen to be. The Tree of **Life**, Tree of **Knowledge**, Tree of **Wisdom**, Tree of **Love**, and the Tree of **Peace**.

KJV Matthew 5: Verse 21

Ye have heard that it was said by them of old time, Thou shalt not kill; and whosoever shall kill shall be in danger of the judgment:

Comment appropriately to "Ye have heard that it was said by them of old time, Thou shalt not kill;"

Jesus Christ is saying, you can recall from the ten commandments given unto Moses; Thou shalt not kill**.**

Comment appropriately to "and whosoever shall kill shall be in danger of the judgment:"

Jesus is making us aware; this commandment still applies even in the New Commandments.

KJV Matthew 5: Verse 22

But I say unto you, That whosoever is angry with his brother without a cause shall be in danger of the judgment: and whosoever shall say to his brother, Raca, shall be in danger of the council: but whosoever shall say, Thou fool, shall be in danger of hell fire.

Comment appropriately to "But I say unto you, That whosoever is angry with his brother without a cause shall be in danger of the judgment:"

Jesus Christ gives light into his New Commandments; this command equals "Love thy neighbor as thyself." Therefore, to hold judgment against your brother shall be in danger of receiving the same conclusion in return.

It would help if you examined your thoughts, intentions, or activities which may lead to karmic effects. In other words, "so shall a man sow, so shall he reap."

Comment appropriately to "and whosoever shall say to his brother, Raca, shall be in danger of the council:"

More importantly, do not call your brother "Raca." It **means** foolish.

Indeed, we all are of one consciousness. And in no way are you not going to be reviewed by the council for this action.

Note: About the **council.** *These* ascended spirit guides, retain higher knowledge and do not take incarnations in most cases to this world.

Comment appropriately to "but whosoever shall say, Thou fool, shall be in danger of hell fire."

You must, albeit calling your brother a fool, because you will bring about torment in your subconscious mind with oneness lies. (God's conscious mind).

Clearly, Jesus is stating that this action shall result in the inner suffering of the mind behind these false statements.

Note: When our Lord refers to fire or, in this case, hell's fire. Try to remember, Christ consciousness is fully awakened! **He has come to destroy lies held in a tormented subconscious human-mind, i.e. (the alter ego-mind).**

KJV Matthew 5: Verse 23

Therefore if thou bring thy gift to the altar, and there rememberest that thy brother hath ought against thee;

Comment appropriately to "Therefore if thou bring thy gift to the altar,"

In this manner, it is the heart we bring forth in Love (gift) to the altar. Our conscious mind gives light to our thoughts, ideas, and desires.

Comment appropriately to "and there rememberest that thy brother hath ought against thee;."

Thus, when you realize you've had non-harmonies interactions with another in exchange disagreements.

KJV Matthew 5: Verse 24

Leave there thy gift before the altar, and go thy way; first be reconciled to thy brother, and then come and offer thy gift.

Comment appropriately to "Leave there thy gift before the altar, and go thy way;"

Leave immediately yet carrying Love within your heart which can lead to the conscious mind of thought.

Comment appropriately to "first be reconciled to thy brother, and then come and offer thy gift."

Next, correct the situation with your brother and then return with Love (gift) and forgiveness to conscious awareness.

KJV Matthew 5: Verse 25

Agree with thine adversary quickly, whiles thou art in the way with him; lest at any time the adversary deliver thee to the judge, and the judge deliver thee to the officer, and thou be cast into prison.

Comment appropriately to "Agree with thine adversary quickly, whiles thou art in the way with him;"

Be sure to recognize in this parable, our Lord's state of being is peaceful. He is affirming to us the way to live and becoming conscious. As a result, to agree with your opposer means that you are allowing for Love to mediate.

Note: Remember, you are allowing God's Holy Spirit to intervene in this segment of unity.

When we surrender ourselves to the Holy Spirit, Love to intercede, essentially, we permit energy to flow through us calmly resulting in more inner strength and power.

Quickly, the adversary is filled with allegiance and finds peace between those who all are present.

Comment appropriately to "lest at any time the adversary deliver thee to the judge,"

Therefore, be aware of your conscious thoughts of compassion because your opposer may become irrational and non-persuasive. Moreover, a peaceful resolution may elude harmoniously.

Comment appropriately to "and the judge deliver thee to the officer, and thou be cast into prison."

When your adversary's conscious *thoughts* are in iniquity, those misdeeds of ideas (evil thoughts) lead to the *subconscious mind* of the alter ego. (Judge delivers you to the officer).

When thoughts and emotions become manifested within the inner workings of your adversary. Things change, or shall we say you will find it difficult to express your point of view at all or in the future?

Lastly, to escape prison, Love, or the usage of the heart may mislead to a non-harmonious solution.

KJV Matthew 5: Verse 26

Verily I say unto thee, Thou shalt by no means come out thence, till thou hast paid the uttermost farthing.

Comment appropriately to "Verily I say unto thee,"

Again, Christ is alerting his Chosen elect on how to enter God's Kingdom.

Comment appropriately to "Thou shalt by no means come out thence, till thou hast paid the uttermost farthing."

Given this parable, Our Lord is saying everyone is allowed to enter the Kingdom of God. Be that as it may, you will pay the total price of consciousness to become sons of God.

KJV Matthew 5: Verse 27

Ye have heard that it was said by them of old time, Thou shalt not commit adultery:

Comment appropriately to "Ye have heard that it was said by them of old time,"

Jesus is referring to the Old Testament, hence the old time.

Comment appropriately to "Thou shalt not commit adultery:"

In the laws of Moses, you were stoned to death in public for committing adultery. The truth to this is the eyewitness of this incident also had to engage in the stoning.

Nonetheless, either the witnesses had bloodshed on their hands, or they had to find you innocent of the crime before the high priest.

KJV Matthew 5: Verse 28

But I say unto you, That whosoever looketh on a woman to lust after her hath committed adultery with her already in his heart.

Comment appropriately to "But I say unto you,"

Jesus is bringing awareness light to his New Commandments.

Comment appropriately to "That whosoever looketh on a woman to lust after her hath committed adultery with her already in his heart."

The inception of this parable brings about conscious thoughts in this state of thinking (looking at a woman with lustful desires).

We have enveloped the ideas leading to emotional conception. In this alter ego state of mind, we bring about deep desires leading to visions within deep thoughts. (Deep passionate thoughts emerge within the subconscious mind by emotions).

When this happens, lustful desires enter the heart. These lustful emotions of darkness manifest between conscious and subconscious minds.

It can, in most cases, ignite the divided mind to uncontrollable behaviors. Therefore, once this emotional state has manifested, the alter ego (human mind) domain enters the darkness.

KJV Matthew 5: Verse 29

And if thy right eye offend thee, pluck it out, and cast *it* from thee: for it is profitable for thee that one of thy members should perish, and not *that* thy whole body should be cast into hell.

Comment appropriately to "And if thy right eye offend thee, pluck it out, and cast *it* from thee:

For starters, this is concerning the spiritual body, not the physical body. The right eye refers to the righteousness of seeing in the spiritual body. Thus, plucking it out is a metaphor for consciously seeing the truth. (By plucking it out is by seeing all facts without judging).

Comment appropriately to "for it is profitable for thee that one of thy members should perish, and not *that* thy whole body should be cast into hell."

All too often, Jesus Christ refers to wealth within the spiritual body. But, again, to remain in this abundance of consciousness, one must *not* allow unrighteous seeing ideas and thoughts to stay.

Contrarily, your spiritual body may retain these lies in a tormented subconscious mind, hence hell's fire.

KJV Matthew 5: Verse 30

And if thy right hand offend thee, cut it off, and cast *it* from thee: for it is profitable for thee that one of thy members should perish, and not *that* thy whole body should be cast into hell.

Comment appropriately to "And if thy right hand offend thee, cut it off, and cast *it* from thee: for it is profitable for thee that one of thy members should perish,

Once more, we are referring to the spiritual body, not the physical body. The right hand refers to the righteousness of the heart in the spiritual body. Therefore, to remain in a wealthy consciousness of Love in the heart.

Metaphorically, cutting and casting away prevents the harming of your spiritual soul, which is always God's will, Love, and truth. However, once the heart is afflicted, all facts can lead to whaling within the soul.

Comment appropriately to "and not *that* thy whole body should be cast into hell."

Most of all, to allow affliction to one's heart torments (*cast to hell*) the soul both consciously and subconsciously. Be that it may, the spiritual meat and bones of truth evade the righteous yearning of Jesus Christ.

KJV Matthew 5: Verse 31

It hath been said, Whosoever shall put away his wife, let him give her a writing of divorcement:

Comment appropriately to "It hath been said, Whosoever shall put away his wife, let him give her a writing of divorcement:"

In the Old Testament Laws given unto Moses, divorces happened because the human flesh manifested. These works of fornication, uncleanness, and backsliding are to reason, to name a few. The wife refers to the mind of a soul.

KJV Matthew 5: Verse 32

But I say unto you, That whosoever shall put away his wife, saving for the cause of fornication, causeth her to commit adultery: and whosoever shall marry her that is divorced committeth adultery.

Comment appropriately to "But I say unto you, That whosoever shall put away his wife, saving for the cause of fornication, causeth her to commit adultery:"

In the New Commandments, to put away; or take on lack of purpose or responsibility for your subconscious mind (*his wife*). In other words, you are causing or exhibiting a lack of faith in the New Teachings of Jesus Christ.

In this lack of faith within the mind, you permit the alter ego-mind (human mind) to become unclean (fornication). Thus, you allow adultery with another inward of the subconscious mind by giving it unrighteous thoughts or shared with the hands of evildoers (causeth her to commit adultery).

The wife can also refer to the conscious mind of the Self—the bridal chamber to the Husbandman. (Refer to Index)

Note: Again, think of your subconscious mind to where all of feelings occur, and memories are stored.

Comment appropriately to "and whosoever shall marry her that is divorced committeth adultery."

Therefore, to enter the altered ego mind (human mind) where impurities stay. It equates to committing adultery within reason. As a spiritual soul, you can not commit adultery in mind. You can retain lies in a tormented human mind.

KJV Matthew 5: Verse 33

Again, ye have heard that it hath been said by them of old time, Thou shalt not forswear thyself, but shalt perform unto the Lord thine oaths:

Comment appropriately to "Again, ye have heard that it hath been said by them of old time,"

Regularly, Christ is replying to scripture written in the First Testament by the teachers of the Law. These old times and testaments shall come to pass upon the completion of the crucifixion.

Comment appropriately to "Thou shalt not forswear thyself, but shalt perform unto the Lord thine oaths:"

The teachers of the law ruled against anyone from saying, I am the Lord. Once more, Jesus Christ is bringing forth light to his new commandments and teachings to us. Thus, we all are of one consciousness.

KJV Matthew 5: Verse 34

But I say unto you, Swear not at all; neither by heaven; for it is God's throne:

Comment appropriately to "But I say unto you,"

If you recall, Jesus always begins his New Commandment to us with this saying. So likewise, this commandment is from the Father, which gives our Lord and Savior a new direction.

Comment appropriately to "Swear not at all; neither by heaven; for it is God's throne:"

We should always avoid swearing because by doing so, we are blaspheming our Father's Love which is in consciousness. We are also harming our soul with these untruths to be mindful of our Father.

For God's throne rests in perfect consciousness.

KJV Matthew 5: Verse 35

Nor by the earth; for it is his footstool: neither by Jerusalem; for it is the city of the great King.

Comment appropriately to "Nor by the earth; for it is his footstool:"

Indeed, earth with a small "e" refers to the inner workings of the intuitive mind. For this reason, Jesus is using a metaphor concerning the mindfulness of the alter-ego (human-mind) as a reference footstool.

Comment appropriately to "neither by Jerusalem; for it is the city of the great King."

Neither Jerusalem takes strengths from knowing the treasures that lie within oneself in understanding the subconscious mind. Thus, the presence (city) of the Father is concerning all things.

The significant amount of wealth greater than Kings is inside one's awareness.

KJV Matthew 5: Verse 36

Neither shalt thou swear by thy head, because thou canst not make one hair white or black.

Comment appropriately to "Neither shalt thou swear by thy head, because thou canst not make one hair white or black."

To swear or affirm thoughts within consciousness can bring harm to the soul's body. Those logical alter-ego thoughts can manifest into the heart-bearing stress beginning with removing inner peace. (Making your hair gray)

By way of explanation, you create stress to accomplish your ambition.

KJV Matthew 5: Verse 37

But let your communication be, Yea, yea; Nay, nay: for whatsoever is more than these cometh of evil.

Comment appropriately to "But let your communication be, Yea, yea; Nay, nay: for whatsoever is more than these cometh of evil."

For this reason, let your answers to questions be with yes, or no. Anything outside of these answers will come from your altered ego (human mind).

When we find reasons to ask questions about someone's intentions, this can distract from a harmonious interaction.

KJV Matthew 5: Verse 38

Ye have heard that it hath been said, An eye for an eye, and a tooth for a tooth:

Comment appropriately to "Ye have heard that it hath been said, An eye for an eye, and a tooth for a tooth:"

In the Old Testament, you have heard an eye that sees all truths and a tooth that understands all realities.

Note: The third eye chakra in all realms of yoga Padma Sana is the eye that sees truths, and the tooth is part of the soul's body that understands nature.

KJV Matthew 5: Verse 39

But I say unto you, That ye resist not evil: but whosoever shall smite thee on thy right cheek, turn to him the other also.

Comment appropriately to "But I say unto you,"

As for the New Testament.

Comment appropriately to "That ye resist not evil: but whosoever shall smite thee on thy right cheek, turn to him the other also."

It would help if you resisted evil expressed verbiage from others' mortal minds. Then, when they unleash their destructive words or actions on you (smite thee), stand on righteousness and by doing so.

You are giving your opposer no inner peace in their ways. In other words, stand on what is right regardless of who it is!

KJV Matthew 5: Verse 40

And if any man will sue thee at the law, and take away thy coat, let him have *thy* cloke also.

Comment appropriately to "And if any man will sue thee at the law, and take away thy coat, let him have *thy* cloke also."

Suppose your brother holds animosity against you in character and takes away his approval of you. Then offer him blessings and forgiveness to your unseen God who sees all things.

KJV Matthew 5: Verse 41

And whosoever shall compel thee to go a mile, go with him twain.

Comment appropriately to "And whosoever shall compel thee to go a mile, go with him twain."

When your antagonist places their evil reasoning on your existence, to prevail in the Lord's teachings. Remain in my peace.

KJV Matthew 5: Verse 42

Give to him that asketh thee, and from him that would borrow of thee turn not thou away.

Comment appropriately to "Give to him that asketh thee,

and from him that would borrow of thee turn not thou away."

Give to your brother what you have more than enough of because I (Your Lord) gave it to you to share. Ask for no payment in return that your gladness be full.

KJV Matthew 5: Verse 43

Ye have heard that it hath been said, Thou shalt love thy neighbour, and hate thine enemy.

Comment appropriately to "Ye have heard that it hath been said,"

You have heard it said before in the Old Testament, formerly known as the First Testament.

Comment appropriately to "Thou shalt love thy neighbour, and hate thine enemy."

In the laws of Moses, you should love your neighbor and disapprove of your enemies.

KJV Matthew 5: Verse 44

But I say unto you, Love your enemies, bless them that curse you, do good to them that hate you, and pray for them which despitefully use you, and persecute you;

Comment appropriately to "But I say unto you,"

As for the New Testament.

Comment appropriately to "Love your enemies,"

Love all who come against you because it is for righteousness, and it is the Father's will. (Love and Truth)

Comment appropriately to "bless them that curse you, do good to them that hate you,"

The teachings of Jesus Christ presence a likeness of the Father. Although we may see this as a commandment of "Thou Shall Not" expression.

We must invite a more profound meaning on how the Lord is advising us to proceed and most importantly, why?

When blessing an individual who despises you, I would like to offer you a Universal principle that Jesus conveys to us.

First, although the alter-ego (human mind) questions the reasoning of offering a blessing, the **Law** of **Giving** and **Receiving,** it is precisely what our Lord intended.

As they say, you only get to keep what you give away! So, by giving away sincerity in a blessing, you are essentially receiving that very same blessing back to yourself.

For example, an individual intentionally denies you access to a reception held for a dear friend.

Although disappointed, you reluctantly reclaim your inward peace, mitigating intuition on the Love you have for Jesus Christ.

Note: In Jesus Christ, there is repose. In the teachings, there is a great deal of abundance and strength.

Just like that, you revel in the forgiveness opposed to the host and rescind thoughts into admiration, prosperity, and abundant joy to their inner workings in Jesus' name.

Also, to do good to those who hate or dislike you is an action of Love and kindness. But be that it may, you can only give away what is inside your heart.

Comment appropriately to "and pray for them which despitefully use you, and persecute you;"

Albeit in the same reasoning of Giving and Receiving; when we pray for others which despite or persecute us!

We are indeed praying for these blessings over our very own lives as well. So, therefore, do this in sincerity!

KJV Matthew 5: Verse 45

That ye may be the children of your Father which is in heaven: for he maketh his sun to rise on the evil and on the good, and sendeth rain on the just and on the unjust.

Comment appropriately to "That ye may be the children of your Father which is in heaven:"

Be cheerful and at rest because you are children of our Father in heaven.

Comment appropriately to "for he maketh his sun to rise on the evil and on the good, and sendeth rain on the just and on the unjust."

Be that it may, our Heavenly Father gives unto each soul four cycles known as seasons of desire. Each of these cycles represents a soul's journey. In other words, for the sun to rise on both evil and good.

A child of God must experience each season on its path to enlightenment. Furthermore, the Father sends rain to indicate the spring season of the desires fulfilled on the just from the unjust; state of being.

Once all desires have been fulfilled, and all understanding is Love and truth. Then, the Self enjoys and recovers oneness in the unity of the child through Christ.

KJV Matthew 5: Verse 46

For if ye love them which love you, what reward have ye? do not even the publicans the same?

Comment appropriately to "For if ye love them which love you, what reward have ye? do not even the publicans the same?"

In the same way, if you Love those who are close to you, and they Love you back very quickly. Then what spiritual growth or knowledge have you learned? Likewise, what have those close to you accomplished?

KJV Matthew 5: Verse 47

And if ye salute your brethren only, what do ye more *than others*? do not even the publicans so?

Comment appropriately to "And if ye salute your brethren only, what do ye more *than others*? do not even the publicans so?"

Even more so, if you "only" acknowledge those close to you as your brother -then what Love and trust are you offering to others? Once again, don't others treat you the same way in this manner?

KJV Matthew 5: Verse 48

Be ye therefore perfect, even as your Father which is in heaven is perfect.

Comment appropriately to "Be ye therefore perfect, even as your Father which is in heaven is perfect."

In conclusion, be of perfection in pursuit of the Kingdom of God. Do not call yourselves into sin yet be of good cheer in your learning on the path to righteousness. For our Father in heaven is of perfect consciousness.

Matthew Chapter 6

KJV Matthew 6: Verse 1

Take heed that ye do not your alms before men, to be seen of them: otherwise ye have no reward of your Father which is in heaven.

Comment appropriately to "Take heed that ye do not your alms before men, to be seen of them:"

Indeed, do not boast before men pridefully your giving, for it shall produce great rewards when done in private. In addition, when sharing, do it from the heart where the Father dwells.

As we begin with the sixth chapter, our Lord is giving us commandments on how to give and receive to enter the Kingdom. But, first, we should be aware of giving other gifts before others.

In this commandment, Christ our Lord is advising the elect to glorify the Father who has graciously given to you more than enough to share!

Comment appropriately to "otherwise ye have no reward of your Father which is in heaven."

Considering this, when we boast before men, we renounce the Father in consciousness.

KJV Matthew 6: Verse 2

Therefore when thou doest *thine* alms, do not sound a trumpet before thee, as the hypocrites do in the synagogues and in the streets, that they may have glory of men. Verily I say unto you, They have their reward.

Comment appropriately to "Therefore when thou doest *thine* alms, do not sound a trumpet before thee, as the hypocrites do in the synagogues and in the streets, that they may have glory of men."

For this reason, make your offering where no one will see what you are doing. Avoid announcing your offering as the deceivers do in the house of worship, tabernacles, and passageways (streets).

Accordingly, they have splendor before men and have allowed the alter-ego (human mind) to receive payment in full, not from heaven.

Comment appropriately to "Verily I say unto you, They have their reward."

The Lord is alerting the elect on how to enter the Kingdom of God. Thus, announcing your pride in earthly riches before others eliminates the purity of heart in consciousness.

KJV Matthew 6: Verse 3

But when thou doest alms, let not thy left hand know what thy right hand doeth:

Comment appropriately to "But when thou doest alms, let not thy left hand know what thy right hand doeth:"

Above all, when you do give to charity or other souls, do it in private. Do not let the spiritual dead (left hand) know what the righteous or spiritually awakened (right hand) is doing.

KJV Mathew 6: Verse 4

That thine alms may be in secret: and thy Father which seeth in secret himself shall reward thee openly.

Comment appropriately to "That thine alms may be in secret: and thy Father which seeth in secret himself shall reward thee openly."

Granted that your giving is in secret, the Father sees all things and shall reward you in the open before others spiritually.

KJV Matthew 6: Verse 5

And when thou prayest, thou shalt not be as the hypocrites *are*: for they love to pray standing in the synagogues and in the corners of the streets, that they may be seen of men. Verily I say unto you, They have their reward.

Comment appropriately to "And when thou prayest, thou shalt not be as the hypocrites *are*: for they love to pray standing in the synagogues and in the corners of the streets, that they may be seen of men."

Furthermore, when you pray, do not follow the spiritually dead because they love praying in the house of worship and holy places—precisely where God's children gather, searching for truths.

Comment appropriately to "Verily I say unto you, They have their reward."

Alert to the elect for entering the Kingdom of God -indeed, not following the teachings of my New Commandments surely can be denied their blessings.

KJV Matthew 6: Verse 6

But thou, when thou prayest, enter into thy closet, and when thou hast shut thy door, pray to thy Father which is in secret; and thy Father which seeth in secret shall reward thee openly.

Comment appropriately to "But thou, when thou prayest, enter into thy closet, and when thou hast shut thy door, pray to thy Father which is in secret; and thy Father which seeth in secret shall reward thee openly."

On the contrary, when you pray, **go within your heart** (enter thy closet) -where no one will disturb you! When you pray, **shut your mouth** (shut the door) thus praying in silence where the mouth and alter-ego mind confuses your thoughts.

Next, pray from the heart where only the Father dwells. Do not pray standing up consequently, from your bending knees for it is honor before God. Believe in your soul without a doubt what you're asking has already been received before the Lord and give thanks in Jesus's name.

KJV Matthew 6: Verse 7

But when ye pray, use not vain repetitions, as the heathen *do*: for they think that they shall be heard for their much speaking.

Comment appropriately to "But when ye pray, use not vain repetitions, as the heathen *do*: for they think that they shall be heard for their much speaking."

Lastly, when you are at prayer, do not use the mouth repeatedly as the spiritually blind and dead.

Because they believe their prayers are answered by asserting their voice.

KJV Matthew 6: Verse 8

Be not ye therefore like unto them: for your Father knoweth what things ye have need of, before ye ask him.

Comment appropriately to "Be not ye therefore like unto them: for your Father knoweth what things ye have need of, before ye ask him."

Therefore, do not be fearful of your asking because your Heavenly Father knows everything before you pray from the heart.

KJV Matthew 6: Verse 9

After this manner therefore pray ye: Our Father which art in heaven, Hallowed be thy name.

Comment appropriately to "After this manner therefore pray ye: Our Father which art in heaven,"

Our only teacher in spirit "Christ" gave us one prayer in his teachings. This can be said with others with the voice or in private in silence. So, pray in this manner:

"Our Father which art in heaven,"

Forever give praise to the Father with Love and Truth in consciousness.

Comment appropriately to "Hallowed be thy name."

Holiness is in thy name.

KJV Matthew 6: Verse 10

Thy kingdom come. Thy will be done in earth, as *it* is in heaven.

Comment appropriately to "Thy kingdom come."

God's Kingdom of shared consciousness becomes for all souls.

Comment appropriately to "Thy will be done in earth, as it is in heaven."

God's will of Love and truth in the subconscious mind. (Notice how it says, *in earth* not on earth). Remember, Mother Earth "Large E" is called Gaia our physical planet.

God's will of Love and truth in the conscious mind. (As it is in heaven)

KJV Matthew 6: Verse 11

Give us this day our daily bread.

Comment appropriately to "Give us this day our daily bread."

Give us today our spiritual nourishment of truths. (Meditation, prayers, uplifting music, and reading scripture are all forms of daily bread).

KJV Matthew 6: Verse 12

And forgive us our debts, as we forgive our debtors.

Comment appropriately to "And forgive us our debts, as we forgive our debtors."

Forgive us of our wrongful thoughts in the subconscious mind. Likewise, forgive others who lend improper thoughts as opposed to me in their subconscious mind.

KJV Matthew 6: Verse 13

And lead us not into temptation, but deliver us from evil: For thine is the kingdom, and the power, and the glory, for ever. Amen.

Comment appropriately to "And lead us not into temptation, but deliver us from evil:"

Do not allow the alter ego human mind to betray our true nature, and let your Love and truth lead us to righteousness.

Comment appropriately to "For thine is the kingdom, and the power, and the glory, for ever. Amen."

For yours is the consciousness, the greatest of all powers, Love, and truth, for all eternity.

Amen (so be it). Forevermore, state of consciousness.

KJV Matthew 6: Verse 14

For if ye forgive men their trespasses, your heavenly Father will also forgive you:

Comment appropriately to "For if ye forgive men their trespasses, your heavenly Father will also forgive you:"

As with (**Matthew 6:12**), Jesus tells us to be (state of mind) compassionate to our brothers or sisters as in Christ. But, unfortunately, those improper thoughts to our opposer can manifest into realized reality.

To forgive as the Father forgives us, we confess our iniquity thoughts toward another for their behavior contrary to you.

Note: Equally important, their behavior may or may not have been intentional against you. So, to release the feelings of hurt, forgive -forgive always and when possible.

KJV Matthew 6: Verse 15

But if ye forgive not men their trespasses, neither will your Father forgive your trespasses.

Comment appropriately to "But if ye forgive not men their trespasses, neither will your Father forgive your trespasses."

In the same manner, if you do not allow for Love and truth from the teachings to forgive. Jesus may withhold the Father's blessings in that event, and your hurt remains as a reminder to allow for Love to intervene.

Note: In some cases, when we're unable to release hurt from others by not forgiving. We may replay these events causing continuous long-suffering to our inner soul and mind. Thus, we essentially bear the pain within ourselves and violate the **Law of Love**.

KJV Matthew 6: Verse 16

Moreover when ye fast, be not, as the hypocrites, of a sad countenance: for they disfigure their faces, that they may appear unto men to fast. Verily I say unto you, They have their reward.

Comment appropriately to "Moreover when ye fast, be not, as the hypocrites, of a sad countenance: for they disfigure their faces, that they may appear unto men to fast."

When you fast, please do not act like those teachers of the Law of Moses who make known their self-righteousness publicly. Instead, they display long faces of their self-sacrifice to men.

For this purpose, let's clarify the difference of a human physical body fast and the teachings of Christ spiritual fast.

First, too fast for the physical body is not spiritual. However, it can provide many benefits that can assist the human body to long-term health and realignment mentally.

Although it's mainly been debated for years by health officials however, in our case. A spiritual fast in done by "being still" for a little while during transcendental meditation.

We fast to rid ourselves of desires in this physical world and its attachments. Thus, renewing of the mind in consciousness.

Comment appropriately to "Verily I say unto you, They have their reward."

Jesus makes us aware of how not to fast in front of others upon entering the Kingdom of God. For they have made their self-sacrifice in the body and not the mind.

KJV Matthew 6: Verse 17

But thou, when thou fastest, anoint thine head, and wash thy face;

Comment appropriately to "But thou, when thou fastest, anoint thine head, and wash thy face;."

(These are the hidden treasures in Jesus Christ's parables)

Accordingly, when you fast, "be still" aligns with your crown chakra (anoint thy head).

The Lord, thy God, will send his Holy Spirit (wash thy face) to and through your circular vortexes of energy cleansing the soul.

Note: If focused our God correctly while in stillness, your tears will surely wash thy face.

KJV Matthew 6: Verse 18

That thou appear not unto men to fast, but unto thy Father which is in secret: and thy Father, which seeth in secret, shall reward thee openly.

Comment appropriately to "That thou appear not unto men to fast,"

Do this form of worship in private, undisturbed, and in truth.

Comment appropriately to "but unto thy Father which is in secret: and thy Father, which seeth in secret, shall reward thee openly."

Subsequently, do this with Love unto the Father in solitude. In this obedience of secrecy, thy God shall reward you openly with wealth from heaven.

KJV Matthew 6: Verse 19

Lay not up for yourselves treasures upon earth, where moth and rust doth corrupt, and where thieves break through and steal:

Comment appropriately to "Lay not up for yourselves treasures upon earth,"

Therefore, resist earthly riches which pass away with the physical body.

Comment appropriately to "where moth and rust doth corrupt, and where thieves break through and steal:"

Furthermore, in the alter-ego (human mind), you resist spiritual truths believing you are the body (rust doth corrupt). Not to mention lies of earthly gains (thieves steal) preventing you from true wealth, spirituality.

KJV Matthew 6: Verse 20

But lay up for yourselves treasures in heaven, where neither moth nor rust doth corrupt, and where thieves do not break through nor steal:

Comment appropriately to "But lay up for yourselves treasures in heaven, where neither moth nor rust doth corrupt, and where thieves do not break through nor steal:."

In truth, store up treasures in consciousness (heaven), where the altered ego (human mind) does not impair. Also, nor can anyone take what is truthful.

KJV Matthew 6: Verse 21

For where your treasure is, there will your heart be also.

Comment appropriately to "For where your treasure is, there will your heart be also."

Once you understand all truths, Love is fully present within the heart.

KJV Matthew 6: Verse 22

The light of the body is the eye: if therefore thine eye be single, thy whole body shall be full of light.

Comment appropriately to "The light of the body is the eye: "

Surrounding this verse and the next, Jesus is bringing light into his teachings. He is stating, the light of the body is the unseen eye within the spiritual body. We are unable to physically see this eye with our human eyes because it is spiritual.

"For it is the third eye or mind's eye that sees all truths. "

In yoga circles, the mind's eye "prana" serves as life force energy.

These are the actual secret teachings of Jesus Christ hidden in parables.

Comment appropriately to "if therefore thine eye be single, thy whole body shall be full of light."

When you can understand all truths, your *eye* will be single. You will radiate light for all to experience.

KJV Matthew 6: Verse 23

But if thine eye be evil, thy whole body shall be full of darkness. If therefore the light that is in thee be darkness, how great *is* that darkness!

Comment appropriately to "But if thine eye be evil, thy

whole body shall be full of darkness."

For if you do not follow my teachings, your eye will remain closed from the light. Also, your body will stay in the spiritual darkness unable to be revealed spiritual truths.

Comment appropriately to "If therefore the light that is in thee be darkness, how great is that darkness!"

For this reason, if your eye does not deliver light, how much darkness do you hold within the subconscious mind?

KJV Matthew 6: Verse 24

No man can serve two masters: for either he will hate the one, and love the other; or else he will hold to the one, and despise the other. Ye cannot serve God and mammon.

Comment appropriately to "No man can serve two masters: for either he will hate the one, and love the other; or else he will hold to the one, and despise the other."

Analogous to this parable, Jesus goes into great depth explaining righteous thought. Indeed, serving two masters creates conflict, which can lead to turbulence in mind.

To make this easier to understand, man either loves earthly riches and remains opposed to spiritual wealth in the heart (he will love the one and hate the other).

Although, obtaining spiritual wealth manifested to earthly wealth is what our Lord intended for his teachings to allow.

Comment appropriately to "Ye cannot serve God and mammon."

In other words, you cannot find God's kingdom seeking after earthly riches first.

Matthew 6:33

But seek ye first the kingdom of God, and his righteousness; and all these things shall be added unto you.

Leaders of the house of worship can receive great benefits from these institutions. However, on the other hand, followers are sometimes unintentionally misled to untruths concerning idea wealth in these ministries. Hence, hold onto one or despise the other.

For this reason, those congregations would greatly benefit in seeking God's Kingdom first and then serving others while allowing for true spiritual wealth to transmute into the manifest.

In other words, place God first in all things, serve others tirelessly, and allow for our Lord and Savior to guide you to earthly riches. Yet, of course, it does take work on one's behalf.

Comment appropriately to "Ye cannot serve God and mammon."

In truth, you cannot serve God and earthly riches.

Note: To obtain wealth, and that's true wealth. You must be in a wealth consciousness state of mind. Reread Matthew 6:33, please.

KJV Matthew 6: Verse 25

Therefore I say unto you, Take no thought for your life, what ye shall eat, or what ye shall drink; nor yet for your body, what ye shall put on. Is not the life more than meat, and the body than raiment?

Comment appropriately to "Therefore I say unto you, Take no thought for your life, what ye shall eat, or what ye shall drink; nor yet for your body, what ye shall put on."

Jesus has given his disciples guidance on how to enter the Kingdom of God.

In essence, think nothing of this physical body, for it is temporary. Our journey upon the planet earth is only for a little while. But be that it may, we owe an outstanding debt to our Father in heaven for this incarnation.

In brief, what you eat is spiritual food. The teachings of God are fruit for the spiritual body coming from the fruit tree, which bears knowledge and understanding.

Otherwise, what shall you drink? The Lord, our God, is this living water, seek his heart, and you'll never thirst again.

Jesus said, "But whosoever drinketh of the water that I shall give him shall never thirst; but the water that I shall give him shall be in him a well of water springing up into everlasting life."

John 4:14

For the body, our collective body is of oneness, the body of

Christ. We all are wearing the same garment of Love and truth.

Our journey here on earth (Mother Earth) is a journey to self-discovery.

Comment appropriately to "Is not the life more than meat, and the body than raiment?"

Because of this, meat refers to the substance or flesh of the spiritual body, which reveals spiritual truth. So, what should you put on like clothing? The spiritual body needs no dress.

We are all made in the image of the Father through the **Universal Law of Oneness**.

KJV Matthew 6: Verse 26

Behold the fowls of the air: for they sow not, neither do they reap, nor gather into barns; yet your heavenly Father feedeth them. Are ye not much better than they?

Comment appropriately to "Behold the fowls of the air: for they sow not, neither do they reap, nor gather into barns;"

Our Lord is leading us to the importance of finding the Kingdom of God within ourselves.

Fowl of the air refers to the emotions in between the conscious and the subconscious mind. Meaning they are within reach of manifest; they require conscious belief (sow not).

Nor do they produce reality because you have not set

intentions on your emotions (Nor do they reap). Furthermore, they do not become a memory to the subconscious mind because you neglect your thoughts (nor gather into barns).

Comment appropriately to "yet your heavenly Father feedeth them. Are ye not much better than they?"

Even so with Love, your Father gives unto your conscious thoughts of abundance. So then why remain unaccepting of what he is allowing you in consciousness of mind (heaven)?

KJV Matthew 6: Verse 27

Which of you by taking thought can add one cubit unto his stature?

Comment appropriately to "Which of you by taking thought can add one cubit unto his stature?"

Jesus is giving light to the presence of oneness in consciousness.

KJV Matthew 6: Verse 28

And why take ye thought for raiment? Consider the lilies of the field, how they grow; they toil not, neither do they spin:

Comment appropriately to "And why take ye thought for raiment? "

In this parable, Jesus is directing his followers to become aware of not worrying about the physical body.

Note: Raiment refers to the physical body, also known as *clothing*. (Race, Gender, Sexuality, or Social Class).

Comment appropriately to "Consider the lilies of the field, how they grow; they toil not, neither do they spin:"

Consider the knowledge (lilies) in the subconscious mind (the field). Expanding (how they grow) conscious thoughts come from your daily experiences on your journey. Remain in my peace (neither do they spin).

KJV Matthew 6: Verse 29

And yet I say unto you, That even Solomon in all his glory was not arrayed like one of these.

Comment appropriately to "And yet I say unto you,"

Furthermore, I call for you to complete the work the Father has given unto you in the Teachings.

Comment appropriately to "That even Solomon in all his glory was not arrayed like one of these."

For in all of Solomon's glory, he did not enter the Kingdom of God as a child.

KJV Matthew 6: Verse 30

Wherefore, if God so clothe the grass of the field, which to day is, and to morrow is cast into the oven, *shall he* not much more *clothe* you, O ye of little faith?

Comment appropriately to "Wherefore, if God so clothe

the grass of the field, which to day is, and to morrow is cast into the oven,"

Indeed, our Father gave the alter-ego (human mind) the day full of pleasure and understanding. Then, tomorrow (next cycle desires), casting out lies (oven or fires) of Love and Truths.

Note: In the scripture, a day refers to the three cycles of desire from the evening, night, and morning. The final cycle is Day, completion of enlightenment.

Comment appropriately to "*shall he* not much more *clothe* you, O ye of little faith?"

For the Father loves you, have faith in Christ.

KJV Matthew 6: Verse 31

Therefore take no thought, saying, What shall we eat? or, What shall we drink? or, Wherewithal shall we be clothed?

Comment appropriately to "Therefore take no thought, saying, What shall we eat? or, What shall we drink? "

For you are children of God, do not worry about the fruits the Christ offers or the water that dwells from within him because he is your provider.

Comment appropriately to "or, Wherewithal shall we be clothed?"

Neither should you concern your thoughts on the physical human body.

KJV Matthew 6: Verse 32

(For after all these things do the Gentiles seek:) for your heavenly Father knoweth that ye have need of all these things.

Comment appropriately to "(For after all these things do the Gentiles seek:) "

After all, the spiritually not awaken and blind seek earthly things.

Comment appropriately to "for your heavenly Father knoweth that ye have need of all these things."

For your heavenly Father sees all things and knows you need them.

KJV Matthew 6: Verse 33

But seek ye first the kingdom of God, and his righteousness; and all these things shall be added unto you.

Comment appropriately to "But seek ye first the kingdom of God, and his righteousness;"

Pursue the Universal oneness mind of the Father (consciousness), which is righteousness in all things.

Comment appropriately to "and all these things shall be added unto you."

A oneness in conscious mind of the Father and anointed by the Holy Spirit. All forms of wealth in the conscious mind of spirit transmute to all wealth periods (including earthly wealth).

KJV Matthew 6: Verse 34

Take therefore no thought for the morrow: for the morrow shall take thought for the things of itself. Sufficient unto the day is the evil thereof.

Comment appropriately to "Take therefore no thought for the morrow: for the morrow shall take thought for the things of itself."

Our Lord, Jesus Christ is stating, rest in my peace, for tomorrow has its own energies and worries. In addition, tomorrow (the morrow) journey of the soul desires will take care of itself.

Comment appropriately to "Sufficient unto the day is the evil thereof."

Additionally, Christ is alerting the disciples on truths concerning entering life's state of being. Acceptable towards the cycle of desires in the subconscious mind.

Matthew Chapter 7

KJV Matthew 7: Verse 1

Judge not, that ye be not judged.

Comment appropriately to "Judge not, that ye be not judged."

In this parable, Yeshua is expanding conscious awareness of inner thoughts seen by our unseen Father in Heaven.

In truth, the altered ego renders judgment subconsciously.

Here's a way to avoid these pitfalls. First, be mindful of your feelings when expressing your thoughts. There is a disharmonious association to vibrational alignment.

Secondly, remember who will judge you according to the measure in which you believe. This Universal principle is a teaching of expression of Love to bring us back into alignment with our true nature.

KJV Matthew 7: Verse 2

For with what judgment ye judge, ye shall be judged: and with what measure ye mete, it shall be measured to you again.

Comment appropriately to "For with what judgment ye judge, ye shall be judged: "

In a like manner, for what or whom you judge will in return judge you likewise.

Note: Before we press on, in principle, when we allow ourselves to judge or have an opinion. We are proceeding into the alter ego (human mind) being (state of mind) heading into karmic implications.

In essence, we are expressing the very thing we are likewise or opposing now of judgment.

Comment appropriately to "and with what measure ye mete, it shall be measured to you again."

In the same way, you will not escape the same amount of judgment you are rending to another. In other words, you are creating karmic effects for your very own lesson, which leads to Love.

KJV Matthew 7: Verse 3

And why beholdest thou the mote that is in thy brother's eye, but considerest not the beam that is in thine own eye?

Comment appropriately to "And why beholdest thou the mote that is in thy brother's eye,"

Therefore, why are you judging your brother's thoughts and actions? In this case, we are not allowing others their free will. Furthermore, he (thy brother) has a mind to use or make their own choices in the same way.

However, in verse three, this parable refers to the mind's eye (seeing all truths) as dull (mote).

Note: In contrast, when expressing our thoughts or desires upon another, we may mistakenly remove the inner workings of Love in the harmonious assertion.

We must remain at peace when others are saying their passions regardless of our thoughts or concerns.

Comment appropriately to "but considerest not the beam that is in thine own eye?"

First, seek all truths in consciousness in your own mind's eye (third eye). The mind's eye (spiritual eye), also known as your third eye, is the eye that sees all truths.

KJV Matthew 7: Verse 4

Or how wilt thou say to thy brother, Let me pull out the mote out of thine eye; and, behold, a beam is in thine own eye?

Comment appropriately to "Or how wilt thou say to thy brother, Let me pull out the mote out of thine eye;"

Consequently, how can you advise your brother spiritually when you haven't discovered all truths within your own mind's eye (third eye).

Comment appropriately to "and, behold, a beam *is* in thine own eye?"

Contrarily, you do not see all truths within your own mind's eye (third eye).

KJV Matthew 7: Verse 5

Thou hypocrite, first cast out the beam out of thine own eye; and then shalt thou see clearly to cast out the mote out of thy brother's eye.

Comment appropriately to "Thou hypocrite, first cast out the beam out of thine own eye;"

You hypocrite, first become aware of your own mind's eye, which sees all truths in the teachings of Jesus Christ.

Comment appropriately to "and then shalt thou see clearly to cast out the mote out of thy brother's eye."

Once you can see all truths within your own mind's eye, then you will become capable of assisting your brother to cast out the light and truths from his third eye.

KJV Matthew 7: Verse 6

Give not that which is holy unto the dogs, neither cast ye your pearls before swine, lest they trample them under their feet, and turn again and rend you.

Comment appropriately to "Give not that which is holy unto the dogs, neither cast ye your pearls before swine, lest they trample them under their feet, and turn again and rend you."

Indeed, do not pass on the teachings of Jesus Christ, (which is holy unto dogs) particularly those who oppose any form of spiritual chat. Neither gives your feelings (pearls) to pigs (those unwilling to accept these teachings), referring to animals (swine - dirty thoughts) in the field (subconscious mind).

Despite this, the pigs alter-ego (human mind) will walk over you, placing you beneath them. Even more so, revoking you over and over if you try again to share the gospels.

KJV Matthew 7: Verse 7

Ask, and it shall be given you; seek, and ye shall find; knock, and it shall be opened unto you:

Comment appropriately to "Ask, and it shall be given you;"

Request, with Love in your heart with no hidden motives, and the Lord thy God will give it in due season.

Comment appropriately to "seek, and ye shall find;"

In all things, search for God, and you will find him.

Comment appropriately to "knock and it shall be opened unto you:"

In your **persistence**, the Lord shall provide away.

KJV Matthew 7: Verse 8

For every one that asketh receiveth; and he that seeketh findeth; and to him that knocketh it shall be opened.

Comment appropriately to "For every one that asketh

receiveth"

In Jesus Christ's new Commandments, there is a way of asking in spirit.

When asking, ask from the heart in silence. Indeed, you shall receive.

Note: When asking for material or earthly matters that are not spiritual. It may take a great deal of patience for your request to manifest.

Honestly, you ask, indeed shall you receive.

Comment appropriately to "and he that seeketh findeth;"

After you have asked from the heart, seek God's abundance of Love in constant gratitude.

Comment appropriately to "and to him that knocketh it shall be opened."

In him which persists in gratitude, the Lord thy God shall make away!

KJV Matthew 7: Verse 9

Or what man is there of you, whom if his son ask bread, will he give him a stone?

Comment appropriately to "Or what man is there of you, whom if his son ask bread, will he give him a stone?"

For what man, small "m" spiritual being; if your child of God asks for spiritual truths (bread) and you give him hurtful insults (stone).

In the above scripture, (Matthew 7: 9), a son asking for bread seeks leaven or spiritual truths from the bread keeper, our Lord Jesus Christ.

Reminder, our Lord Jesus speaks to those seeking him in spirituality all the time.

KJV Matthew 7: Verse 10

Or if he ask a fish, will he give him a serpent?

Comment appropriately to "Or if he ask a fish, will he give him a serpent?"

Nonetheless, if your son shall ask for the teachings (fish) of Jesus Christ and you provide him with unrighteous untruths (serpent) that lead him to the grapevine (instructions outside of the New Testament).

KJV Matthew 7: Verse 11

If ye then, being evil, know how to give good gifts unto your children, how much more shall your Father which is in heaven give good things to them that ask him?

Comment appropriately to "if ye then, being evil, know how to give good gifts unto your children,"

Indeed, if you live in a divided mind (the alter-ego), understand how to give Love to your followers, close friends, and family.

Comment appropriately to "how much more shall your Father which is in heaven give good things to them that ask him?"

How much more will the 'Good Man" who is our Father deliver to his children that ask him in abundance?

KJV Matthew 7: Verse 12

Therefore all things whatsoever ye would that men should do to you, do ye even so to them: for this is the law and the prophets.

Comment appropriately to "Therefore all things whatsoever ye would that men should do to you, do ye even so to them:"

In the same manner, whatever you would have a brother pray and believe for you, pray, and believe for him likewise.

Comment appropriately to "for this is the law and the prophets."

Indeed, this was so even before the laws of Moses.

KJV Matthew 7: Verse 13

Enter ye in at the strait gate: for wide is the gate, and broad is the way, that leadeth to destruction, and many there be which go in thereat:

Comment appropriately to "Enter ye in at the strait gate: for wide *is* the gate, and broad is the way, that leadeth to destruction,"

Therefore, to enter God's Kingdom, Love and truths are realized (straight gate). Thus, living in a divided mind (wide is the gate) of poverty and unrighteousness leads to destruction in the heart.

Comment appropriately to "and many there be which go in threat:"

With the result that you do not follow the teachings of Jesus Christ our Lord, many will not enter the Kingdom of God.

KJV Matthew 7: Verse 14

Because strait *is* the gate, and narrow is the way, which leadeth unto life, and few there be that find it.

Comment appropriately to "Because strait *is* the gate, and narrow *is* the way, which leadeth unto life,"

Furthermore, guidance by God's Holy Spirit (strait is the gate) is the way, and thereof is enlightenment which leads to eternal light and life.

Comment appropriately to "and few there be that find it."

Nevertheless, only the Chosen elect will find it.

KJV Matthew 7: Verse 15

Beware of false prophets, which come to you in sheep's clothing, but inwardly they are ravening wolves.

Comment appropriately to "Beware of false prophets, which come to you in sheep's clothing,"

Please keep your eyes out for those unwilling to accept (false prophets) the teachings of Jesus Christ; they come against you from many different religions (sheep's clothing), beliefs, and generational traditions.

Comment appropriately to "but inwardly they are ravening wolves."

Moreover, inwardly, they are serpents and will revile against you without reason.

KJV Matthew 7: Verse 16

Ye shall know them by their fruits. Do men gather grapes of thorns, or figs of thistles?

Comment appropriately to "Ye shall know them by their fruits."

More importantly, you will recognize them by their thoughts and behaviors, which come from their heart.

Comment appropriately to "Do men gather grapes of thorns, or figs of thistles?"

Wherefore, do righteous men seek unrighteous thoughts amongst honest spiritual teachings?

KJV Matthew 7: Verse 17

Even so every good tree bringeth forth good fruit; but a corrupt tree bringeth forth evil fruit.

Comment appropriately to "Even so every good tree

bringeth forth good fruit;"

Even more so, every elect who does not deviate from the teachings of Jesus shall bring forth sincerity (good fruit) from the heart.

Comment appropriately to "but a corrupt tree bringeth forth evil fruit."

More so, everyone who neglects the truths (corrupt tree) in the teachings of Christ shall remain in the darkness of their divided mind withholding Love.

KJV Matthew 7: Verse 18

A good tree cannot bring forth evil fruit, neither can a corrupt tree bring forth good fruit.

Comment appropriately to "A good tree cannot bring forth evil fruit,"

In truth, the elect who follows the teachings accordingly cannot bring forth unrighteousness.

Comment appropriately to "neither *can* a corrupt tree bring forth good fruit."

Similarly, an unrighteous divided mind (portraying good or evil) cannot bring forth righteous thinking.

KJV Matthew 7: Verse 19

Every tree that bringeth not forth good fruit is hewn down, and cast into the fire.

Comment appropriately to "Every tree that bringeth not forth good fruit is hewn down, and cast into the fire."

Consequently, every unrighteous truth outside of Jesus' New Testament shall be brought downward and rejected within the subconscious mind (alter ego human mind).

KJV Matthew 7: Verse 20

Wherefore by their fruits ye shall know them.

Comment appropriately to "Wherefore by their fruits ye shall know them."

For this reason, you will know them by their truths (fruits) because they accepted my new commandments.

KJV Matthew 7: Verse 21

Not every one that saith unto me, Lord, Lord, shall enter into the kingdom of heaven; but he that doeth the will of my Father which is in heaven.

Comment appropriately to "Not every one that saith unto me, Lord, Lord, shall enter into the kingdom of heaven;"

Indeed, I tell you, not every person who calls upon the Lord Jesus shall be anointed by the Holy Spirit in consciousness.

Comment appropriately to "but he that doeth the will of my Father which is in heaven."

More importantly, only those who accept and do the teachings from the Father in consciousness shall enter.

KJV Matthew 7: Verse 22

Many will say to me in that day, Lord, Lord, have we not prophesied in thy name? and in thy name have cast out devils? and in thy name done many wonderful works?

Comment appropriately to "Many will say to me in that day, Lord, Lord, have we not prophesied in thy name?"

Likewise, many followers of Christ will say in the day, Lord, did you not see me glorifying thy name in the house of worship?

Comment appropriately to "and in thy name done many wonderful works?"

In like manner, pray, uplift, and harmonize music passionately in thy name?

Comment appropriately to "and in thy name have cast out devils? and in thy name done many wonderful works?"

Furthermore, I witnessed, attended service faithfully, and prayed for others in thy name?

KJV Matthew 7: Verse 23

And then will I profess unto them, I never knew you: depart from me, ye that work iniquity.

Comment appropriately to "And then will I profess unto them, I never knew you: depart from me, ye that work iniquity."

Therefore, thy Lord Jesus will proclaim before God the Father, depart from me. I never knew you because you sought out unrighteous worship and disobeyed my commandments.

KJV Matthew 7: Verse 24

Therefore whosoever heareth these sayings of mine, and doeth them. I will liken him unto a wise man, which built his house upon a rock:

Comment appropriately to "Therefore whosoever heareth these sayings of mine, and doeth them,"

For this reason, whoever obeys my new commandments and does the work from the Father shall keep truths in the heart.

Comment appropriately to "I will liken him unto a wise man, which built his house upon a rock:"

Likewise, I will know him to be a chosen elect, and in his obedience, the anointed will complete his soul (house) with truths (rock).

KJV Matthew 7: Verse 25

And the rain descended, and the floods came, and the winds blew, and beat upon that house; and it fell not: for it was founded upon a rock.

Comment appropriately to "And the rain descended, and the floods came, and the winds blew, and beat upon that house; and it fell not:"

Indeed, the storms of doubt shall descend upon you, then your emotions (floods or water) will leave questions or confusion. Followed by disbelief (winds) yet instill (stillness) the soul full of truths will stand.

Comment appropriately to "and it fell not:"

Above all, the soul (spiritual body) stood on truths.

KJV Matthew 7: Verse 26

And every one that heareth these sayings of mine, and doeth them not, shall be likened unto a foolish man, which built his house upon the sand:

Comment appropriately to "And every one that heareth these sayings of mine, and doeth them not, shall be likened unto a foolish man,"

Every person that hears my words of Love and truth and does not follow my teachings. I shall consider him an evildoer of unrighteousness.

Comment appropriately to "which built his house upon the sand:"

Nonetheless, these men filled their soul (house) with untruths, and it is not at rest.

KJV Matthew 7: Verse 27

And the rain descended, and the floods came, and the winds blew, and beat upon that house; and it fell: and great was the fall of it.

Comment appropriately to "And the rain descended, and the floods came, and the winds blew, and beat upon that house;"

Thus, the storms of doubt shall descend upon him, then the emotions (floods or water) will leave turbulence in mind. Moreover, disbelief (winds) will leave reluctance in the mind because this house has no truths to stand on.

Comment appropriately to "and it fell: and great was the fall of it."

Furthermore, without truths, man's spirit falls before men because of immorality and falsehoods.

Matthew Chapter 8

KJV Matthew 8: Verse 3

And Jesus put forth *his* hand, and touched him, saying, I will; be thou clean. And immediately, his leprosy was cleansed.

Comment appropriately to "I will; be thou clean."

Clearly, in this verse, Jesus is performing one of his many miracles. But, by doing so, Jesus is showing his everlasting Love by stating, "I will."

In each moment of our day, our Lord God constantly presents his will to each of us. Therefore, we must become more mindful of his presence within our daily lives.

When you slow down and take a moment to notice simple things such as your breathing, you become more in tune with who you are in spirit. In essence, "Be thou clean" is a state of being.

KJV Matthew 8: Verse 4

And Jesus saith unto him, See thou tell no man; but go thy way, shew thyself to the priest, and offer the gift that Moses commanded, for a testimony unto them.

Comment appropriately to "See thou tell no man; but go thy way, shew thyself to the priest,"

Our Messiah gives the priest away to accept the teachings of Christ that abolish their evilness. Hence, in the manifest of these miracles, thus, the "cleansing of leprosy."

Regarding our Lord, he commands the cleansed soul to go in peace (go thy way); however, be that it may, it had become a testament to the Lord's Love of cleansing to bear witness (show thyself) before the high priest.

Comment appropriately to "and offer the gift that Moses commanded, for a testimony unto them."

In haste, the cleansed soul offered the **truth** (Moses commanded) of Jesus' miracle as the Messiah, which is here in ending all suffering in the mind.

KJV Matthew 8: Verse 7

And Jesus saith unto him, I will come and heal him.

Comment appropriately to "I will come and heal him."

"I will come and heal him" in this parable, which comes out of context in verse six of a request. In essence, the healer (Lord God) heals the soul upon request. You are one with it being the state of mind.

You may freely ask in spirit for healing from it. (In consciousness)

Note: In many cases of healing, the mind is where all forms of illnesses develop. When we understand we are spirit (mind) and not the body (alter-ego). We can begin to see how the mind creates or identifies an initial sickness.

Hence, heal the mind, and the body will follow suit.

KJV Matthew 8: Verse 10

When Jesus heard *it*, he marvelled, and said to them that followed, Verily I say unto you, I have not found so great faith, no, not in Israel.

Comment appropriately to "Verily I say unto you, I have not found so great faith, no, not in Israel."

The Lord's state of being was Self-realization (fully awakened and anointed by the Holy Spirit), Jesus remained in full consciousness. In other words, Jesus could see all states of everyone's consciousness, beliefs, thoughts, and a soul's heart in spirit.

So, for our Lord and Savior to make this statement meant he saw beyond what the human eyes could understand. The **centurion** (pronounced cen-TU-ri-un) roman soldier leader had great faith and belief in Christ as God.

As with faith, any prayers you believe within the heart. If you fully accept, indeed, you shall receive the very blessing of your asking!

KJV Matthew 8: Verse 11

And I say unto you, That many shall come from the east and

west, and shall sit down with Abraham, and Isaac, and Jacob, in the kingdom of heaven.

Comment appropriately to "And I say unto you, That many shall come from the east and west,"

These are the truths on entering the Kingdom of God. Many children of God have accepted the teachings of Jesus Christ both far and near.

Comment appropriately to "and shall sit down with Abraham, and Isaac, and Jacob, in the kingdom of heaven."

Shall become of one conscious in the Father of Abraham, Isaac, and Jacob in consciousness.

KJV Matthew 8: Verse 12

But the children of the kingdom shall be cast out into outer darkness: there shall be weeping and gnashing of teeth.

Comment appropriately to "But the children of the kingdom shall be cast out into outer darkness:"

Children opposed to the teachings in the new commandments shall be outcasted and remain in the darkness in the subconscious mind.

Comment appropriately to "there shall be weeping and gnashing of teeth."

By their defiance of the teachings, at the end of days. Therefore, there will be wailing and deep mourning of a soul's misdeeds.

KJV Matthew 8: Verse 13

And Jesus said unto the centurion, Go thy way; and as thou hast believed, *so* be it done unto thee. And his servant was healed in the selfsame hour.

Comment appropriately to "Go thy way; and as thou hast believed, *so* be it done unto thee."

As a result of your heart having faith believing in Christ, go your way, your acceptance of truth has made your request manifest.

KJV Matthew 8: Verse 20

And Jesus saith unto him, The foxes have holes, and the birds of the air *have* nests; but the Son of man hath not where to lay *his* head.

Comment appropriately to "The foxes have holes, and the birds of the air *have* nests;"

About foxes have their holes; this hypocrite goes and hides from all forms of spiritual truths and covers them with lies. In other words, this soul chooses to ignore truths that lies within them. The "I" in "I am" hence, leans on material goods that die with the body. Thus, the birds of the air (ideas and thoughts in the subconscious mind).

However, in this case, birds of the air have nests; -expands on the notion that a person has everything they need material-wealth, including ignorance or not pursuing Love and truth which eternal.

Comment appropriately to "but the Son of man hath not where to lay *his* head."

Therefore, the Son of man, large "S" refers to Christ, has no place to lay his burdens because of the world's long-suffering. In short, the Lord is about his Father's business and lives by Love and truth of righteousness.

Remember when I said this earlier; "we will all eventually get there." By the grace of God!

KJV Matthew 8: Verse 22

But Jesus said unto him, Follow me; and let the dead bury their dead.

Comment appropriately to "Follow me; let the dead bury their dead."

Jesus is commanding us all to; "Follow me." Indeed, do not deviate from the teachings which bear fruit into everlasting life. Also, let the spiritually not aware bury one another with their unrighteous thinking.

KJV Matthew 8: Verse 26

And he saith unto them, Why are ye fearful, O ye of little faith? Then he arose and rebuked the winds and the sea; and there was a great calm.

Comment appropriately to "Why are ye fearful, O ye of little faith?"

In truth, our Lord God sees all things, so the pertinent

question to you is faith. "Why are ye fearful?" In our daily lives, we face difficult choices and decisions. Moreover, we develop our lives with how we react to worldly events.

In other words, we take on fear which our Father in heaven did not give to us!

When we fear, we attract the very thing we fear. Thus, we must experience the "cause and effect" or, hence, karmic lesson. Our minds surround these principles, and to avoid doing the Father's work through Jesus Christ is an unacceptable approach and violation of God's will.

KJV Matthew 8: Verse 32

And he said unto them, Go. And when they came out, they went into the herd of swine: and behold, the whole herd of swine ran violently down a steep place into the sea and perished in the waters.

Comment appropriately to "Go."

In righteousness, go, wherefore free thy mind in the subconscious.

Matthew Chapter 9

KJV Matthew 9: verse 2

And, behold, they brought to him a man sick of the palsy, lying on a bed: and Jesus seeing their faith said unto the sick of the palsy; Son, be of good cheer; thy sins be forgiven thee.

Comment appropriately to "Son, be of good cheer; thy sins be forgiven thee."

As we begin in the ninth chapter of Matthew, the Messiah begins fulfilling the scriptures of a Lord who was to come and end all suffering. Momentarily, Jesus is commanding one of his sheep to be grateful for their forgiveness of sins.

In like manner, our sins are forgiven by the blood of our Lord and Savior upon our humble request.

KJV Matthew 9: verse 4

And Jesus knowing their thoughts said, Wherefore think ye evil in your hearts?

Comment appropriately to "Wherefore think ye evil in your hearts?"

In truth, our Lord Jesus sees all men's hearts; therefore, all evil falls from the alter-ego subconscious mind. In short, evil thoughts arrive from wrongful thinking and then transmute their way into evil deeds extending to the heart.

KJV Matthew 9: verse 5

For whether is easier, to say, *Thy* sins be forgiven thee; or to say, Arise, and walk?

Comment appropriately to "For whether is easier, to say, *Thy* sins be forgiven thee; or to say, Arise, and walk?"

To this end, being one in the Father, Christ is anointed by the Holy Spirit and can say, truly your sins are forgiven. Given power from the Father in heaven, awaken and be in your gladness.

KJV Matthew 9: verse 6

But that ye may know that the Son of man hath power on earth to forgive sins, (then saith he to the sick of the palsy,) Arise, take up thy bed, and go unto thine house.

Comment appropriately to "But that ye may know that the Son of man hath power on earth to forgive sins,"

In the likeness of the Father, and in one accord, I have come in the manifest (Son of man) to forgive this generation's sins forever.

Comment appropriately to "Arise, take up thy bed, and go unto thine house."

Enlightenment, take up your cross in the same manner of Christ bearing all wrongful deeds. Cleanse the soul (house) with the purity of heart.

KJV Matthew 9: verse 9

And as Jesus passed forth from thence, he saw a man, named Matthew, sitting at the receipt of custom: and he saith unto him, Follow me. And he arose, and followed him.

Comment appropriately to "Follow me"

Consequently, this is what our Savior intended for us all and that is, "follow me." Therefore, do not deviate from the teachings of Christ our Lord through transcendental meditation, mindfulness of being still—manifest Love and truth within the heart.

KJV Matthew 9: verse 12

But when Jesus heard *that*, he said unto them, They that be whole need not a physician, but they that are sick.

Comment appropriately to "They that be whole need not a physician, but they that are sick."

Although the Messiah is conveying this to the Pharisees (Church leaders). In essence, those who do the work given from the Father remain in the wholeness body of Christ.

However, those that chose not to follow the teachings of Christ shall live in the sickness of a divided mind. So, he will remain without peace.

KJV Matthew 9: verse 13

But go ye and learn what *that* meaneth, I will have mercy, and not sacrifice: for I am not come to call the righteous, but sinners to repentance.

Comment appropriately to "But go ye and learn what *that* meaneth, I will have mercy, and not sacrifice:"

Meanwhile, to conclude verse twelve. Jesus leads the Pharisees to obtain his guidance from the Father most worthy of the gospels. Hence, he challenges them to seek truths from his teachings.

Jesus came into manifest not to atone sins; yet to give mercy. Try to remember when one proceeds into compassion, is to find, Love and peace. Regardless of if one is giving or receiving it, in any case, it leads to understanding.

Comment appropriately to "for I am not come to call the righteous, but sinners to repentance."

For Jesus, did not come for those who follow the laws of Moses believing they are righteous. Therefore, even though they walk in darkness of understanding, I (Christ) manifested to receive the repentance of a genuine heart to follow my way of worship.

KJV Matthew 9: verse 15

And Jesus said unto them, Can the children of the bridechamber mourn, as long as the bridegroom is with them? but the days will come, when the bridegroom shall be taken from them, and then shall they fast.

Comment appropriately to "Can the children of the bridechamber mourn, as long as the bridegroom is with them?"

Indeed, can my disciples (bridechamber) yearn (mourn) and desire for their Lord's (bridegroom) consciousness forthwith that gives understanding, Love, and truths?

Comment appropriately to "but the days will come, when the bridegroom shall be taken from them, and then shall they fast."

Likewise, soon my disciples will search for their perfect consciousness (Christ) which shall give of its life for all. On that occasion, then shall they take a break (fast) from the world's troubles.

Note: **Too fast in spirit** (not in the body) is done by **transcendental meditation**. These are the works given to us by our Father in heaven. We must learn to "be still" for a little while **(Jesus' teachings)** to receive guidance to the kingdom.

KJV Matthew 9: verse 16

No man putteth a piece of new cloth unto an old garment, for that which is put in to fill it up taketh from the garment, and the rent is made worse.

Comment appropriately to "No man putteth a piece of new cloth unto an old garment,"

Furthermore, no soul excepts the new teachings (piece of new cloth) that likes the gathering of long suffering within their being (body - cloth). Nor, hurtful words of unrighteous thoughts (old garments) or guilt held in the subconscious mind.

Comment appropriately to "for that which is put in to fill it up taketh from the garment, and the rent is made worse."

Those unrighteous reflections weigh down torment (put in to fill up) on the subconscious mind (garment) in return, place sickness on the physical body (rent or held guilt), and, if left alone, persist -worsen.

KJV Matthew 9: verse 17

Neither do men put new wine into old bottles: else the bottles break, and the wine runneth out, and the bottles perish: but they put new wine into new bottles, and both are preserved.

Comment appropriately to "Neither do men put new wine into old bottles: else the bottles break, and the wine runneth out, and the bottles perish: "

On the contrary, a believer in the teachings of Christ (new wine) will not follow the Laws of Moses (old bottles). Otherwise, he will not align with the spiritual truths in mind (bottles break).

Thus, the new commandments do not hold within consciousness (wine runneth out) because it ruins all forms of Love and Truth (bottles perish) in the subconsciousness.

Comment appropriately to "but they put new wine into new bottles, and both are preserved."

Therefore, when the New Commandments (new wine) advance in the new teachings (new bottles), both leadeth to the Kingdom of God (preserved).

KJV Matthew 9: verse 22

But Jesus turned him about, and when he saw her, he said, Daughter, be of good comfort; thy faith hath made thee whole. And the woman was made whole from that hour.

Comment appropriately to "Daughter, be of good comfort; thy faith hath made thee whole."

For the Holy Spirit, Woman (daughter) take comfort; belief has made you whole by faith in Christ Jesus our Lord.

KJV Matthew 9: verse 24

He said unto them, Give place: for the maid is not dead, but sleepeth. And they laughed him to scorn.

Comment appropriately to "Give place: for the maid is not dead, but sleepeth."

Peace, be still (Give place), for thy daughter is not dead in spirit says the Lord thy God, for she is only sleeping (not spiritually awoken).

KJV Matthew 9: verse 28

And when he was come into the house, the blind men came

to him: and Jesus saith unto them, Believe ye that I am able to do this? They said unto him, Yea, Lord.

Comment appropriately to "Believe ye that I am able to do this?

Do you believe within your heart, soul, and mind that I am able?

KJV Matthew 9: verse 29

Then touched he their eyes, saying, According to your faith be it unto you.

Comment appropriately to "According to your faith be it unto you"

Confer, without doubt, your faith has healed you.

KJV Matthew 9: verse 30

And their eyes were opened; and Jesus straitly charged them, saying, See *that* no man know *it*.

Comment appropriately to "See *that* no man know *it*."

Make your awareness on the evildoers who will come against you as non-believers.

KJV Matthew 9: verse 37

Then saith he unto his disciples, The harvest truly *is* plenteous, but the labourers *are* few;

Comment appropriately to "The harvest truly *is* plenteous, but the labourers *are* few;"

At this moment, there are many followers of Christ searching for truths (harvest), yet the workers who are authorized to teach my New Testament are few.

KJV Matthew 9: verse 38

Pray ye therefore the Lord of the harvest, that he will send forth labourers into his harvest.

Comment appropriately to "Pray ye therefore the Lord of the harvest, that he will send forth labourers into his harvest."

Thus, give thanks unto the Lord of all, ask that he grant additional Love into the gathering of Christ Jesus disciples.

Matthew Chapter 10

KJV Matthew 10: verse 5

These twelve Jesus sent forth, and commanded them, saying, Go not into the way of the Gentiles, and into *any* city of the Samaritans enter ye not:

Comment appropriately to "These twelve Jesus sent forth, and commanded them, saying, Go not into the way of the Gentiles, and into *any* city of the Samaritans enter ye not:"

The twelve disciples received guidance from our Lord as he commanded them by saying. Go before all men (Gentiles) and enter their presence (city).

Where non-believer will enter and spread the gospel of the Lord to end all suffering.

KJV Matthew 10: verse 6

But go rather to the lost sheep of the house of Israel.

Comment appropriately to "But go rather to the lost sheep of the house of Israel."

In addition, go before those in the house of worship specifically seeking out followers (lost sheep) of Christ. Notwithstanding, because their souls seek truths in finding the kingdom.

KJV Matthew 10: verse 7

And as ye go, preach, saying, The kingdom of heaven is at hand.

Comment appropriately to "And as ye go, preach, saying, The kingdom of heaven is at hand."

Therefore, as you go, crying out (preach) with your mouth boldly and confessing without fear that the kingdom of heaven is in your heart (at hand).

KJV Matthew 10: verse 8

Heal the sick, cleanse the lepers, raise the dead, cast out devils: freely ye have received, freely give.

Comment appropriately to "Heal the sick, cleanse the lepers, raise the dead, cast out devils: freely ye have received, freely give."

Thus, healing the sick in the subconscious mind cleansing out the guilt held within, awaken the spiritually dead, cast out false doctrine with the Holy Spirit.

Indeed, freely you have received by the Father. Now freely give to all who ask for assistance in spirit.

KJV Matthew 10: verse 9

Provide neither gold, nor silver, nor brass in your purses,

Comment appropriately to "Provide neither gold, nor silver, nor brass in your purses,"

Rely not on your subconscious emotions or memories (gold nor silver) of what has passed (purse).

KJV Matthew 10: verse 10

Nor scrip for *your* journey, neither two coats, neither shoes, nor yet staves: for the workman is worthy of his meat.

Comment appropriately to "Nor scrip for *your* journey, neither two coats, neither shoes, nor yet staves:"

Thus, for the (soul's) journey, take nothing to write down or memorize; for the Holy Spirit will speak on your behalf because it is given by spirit. Take righteous ideas and not unrighteous thoughts (two coats); loosen your sandals (neither shoe) into communion with others in oneness.

Lastly, do not take unrighteous humanity's belief (staves) to anyone because we all are one in the body of Christ!

Comment appropriately to "for the workman is worthy of his meat."

As a result of your Love in Christ, you shall receive flesh of the spiritual body (meat) that reveals spiritual truth.

KJV Matthew 10: verse 11

And into whatsoever city or town ye shall enter, enquire who in it is worthy; and there abide till ye go thence.

Comment appropriately to "And into whatsoever city or town ye shall enter, enquire who in it is worthy;"

For whomever you sit in the presence (city or town) of another, ask the person to understand Jesus Christ, our Lord and Savior.

Comment appropriately to "and there abide till ye go thence."

Therefore, if Love and truth are receptive, stay there with an open heart in communion.

KJV Matthew 10: verse 12

And when ye come into an house, salute it.

Comment appropriately to "And when ye come into an house, salute it."

Furthermore, once you become harmonious with another soul (house), bless the divinity (salute it) within them.

KJV Matthew 10: verse 13

And if the house be worthy, let your peace come upon it: but if it be not worthy, let your peace return to you.

Comment appropriately to "And if the house be worthy, let your peace come upon it:"

For this reason, if the soul is receptive (worthy) to the teachings of Jesus Christ, allow your Love to be in oneness in spirit.

Comment appropriately to "but if it be not worthy, let your peace return to you."

However, if one's soul is not receptive to the teachings of Christ within, allow your Love to remain within your heart. Thus, allowing that soul their "free will" of choice.

KJV Matthew 10: verse 14

And whosoever shall not receive you, nor hear your words, when ye depart out of that house or city, shake off the dust of your feet.

Comment appropriately to "And whosoever shall not receive you, nor hear your words, when ye depart out of that house or city,"

Again, whoever is not welcoming to you in spirit or does not care to hear the gospels on the teachings, then vacate their presence and allow their soul to be at peace.

Comment appropriately to "shake off the dust of your feet."

Remain in my peace (shake off the dust) and do not allow their choice to disturb you on your journey (feet).

KJV Matthew 10: verse 15

Verily I say unto you, It shall be more tolerable for the land of Sodom and Gomorrha in the day of judgment, than for that city.

Comment appropriately to "Verily I say unto you, It shall be more tolerable for the land of Sodom and Gomorrha in the day of judgment, than for that city."

Truly I give my disciples reasons on how to enter God's kingdom. It would be more allowable than genuine faith before Jesus Christ (tolerable). Rather than being in the presence (city) of those being near the Kingdom of God.

Moreover, Christ is the cornerstone of the New Commandments and the teachings. Meaning, he has authority to *judge all; however, he will not* do so because of Love and truth.

Note: The land Sodom and Gomorrah represent the subconscious mind of adulterous thoughts and pridefulness. These disharmonious reflections (low vibrations) may manifest into evil deeds thus not allowing Love or purity which will not enable one to enter God's kingdom.

Surely, Love and truth is what's necessary of God's will for entering.

KJV Matthew 10: verse 16

Behold, I send you forth as sheep in the midst of wolves: be ye therefore wise as serpents, and harmless as doves.

Comment appropriately to "Behold, I send you forth as sheep in the midst of wolves:"

Likewise, I send you into the world as my faithful (sheep) amongst the unbelievers (wolves).

Comment appropriately to "be ye therefore wise as serpents, and harmless as doves."

Thus, on this account, become aware of the unrighteous (serpents) and the unjust because of their adulterous ways. Therefore, rest in my peace, do not harm your brother or sister, and be as peacemakers (doves).

KJV Matthew 10: verse 17

But beware of men: for they will deliver you up to the councils, and they will scourge you in their synagogues;

Comment appropriately to "But beware of men: for they will deliver you up to the councils, and they will scourge you in their synagogues;"

However, become aware of evildoers who have not accepted the teachings of Jesus Christ by gathering their understanding from old scripture. Once they challenge your way of worship, they'll revile you in their subconscious mind (councils).

Some may even renounce your way of worship in the house of prayer (synagogues).

KJV Matthew 10: verse 18

And ye shall be brought before governors and kings for my sake, for a testimony against them and the Gentiles.

Comment appropriately to "And ye shall be brought before governors and kings for my sake,"

Afterward, you may be brought before other non-believers (governors) in the teachings of Christ or leaders (kings) in the house of Worship and tabernacles for Jesus' sake.

Comment appropriately to "for a testimony against them and the Gentiles."

Thus, to refute your way of believing and to those leading the church (Gentiles).

Note: About the Gentiles, we rest in knowing this meaning is in trust of Love. It is the body of work that Christ refers to the church, which represents all souls in the kingdom of Heaven.

KJV Matthew 10: verse 19

But when they deliver you up, take no thought how or what ye shall speak: for it shall be given you in that same hour what ye shall speak.

Comment appropriately to "But when they deliver you up, take no thought how or what ye shall speak:"

Nonetheless, when they accuse you within their subconscious mind, remain in peace and say nothing in your defense. For it is the Holy Spirit that will intervene.

Comment appropriately to "for it shall be given you in that same hour what ye shall speak."

At this moment, lean not to your understanding of what's spirits desires are for your opposer. For it is the Holy Spirit which speaks on your behalf. Therefore, allow this by remaining within me (Jesus Christ).

KJV Matthew 10: verse 20

For it is not ye that speak, but the Spirit of your Father which speaketh in you.

Comment appropriately to "For it is not ye that speak, but the Spirit of your Father which speaketh in you."

Furthermore, it is not you that speaks words of Love. In this obedience of surrendering, it is the Holy Spirit that speaks from the Father which transmutes Love and truth to your opposer in Christ's name.

KJV Matthew 10: verse 21

And the brother shall deliver up the brother to death, and the father the child: and the children shall rise up against *their* parents, and cause them to be put to death.

Comment appropriately to "And the brother shall deliver up the brother to death, and the father the child:"

Hence, the evil subconscious mind of your opposer shall place his very own soul in darkness (death) in the alter-ego (human mind), giving birth (child) as the Father to inner anger.

Comment appropriately to "and the children shall rise up against *their* parents, and cause them to be put to death."

Thus, the birth (inner anger) alludes to negative energy rages (against the parents). Then places inwardly the subconsciousness to hell-like fires of a lie of destruction (put to death). Thus, will enrage more and more until peace can be obtained within.

KJV Matthew 10: verse 22

And ye shall be hated of all *men* for my name's sake: but he that endureth to the end shall be saved.

Comment appropriately to "And ye shall be hated of all *men* for my name's sake: but he that endureth to the end shall be saved."

Because of me, your Lord God, men shall bring hatred against you for the sake of truth; however, my disciples will endure to the end and shall be delivered.

KJV Matthew 10: verse 23

But when they persecute you in this city, flee ye into another: for verily I say unto you, Ye shall not have gone over the cities of Israel, till the Son of man be come.

Comment appropriately to "But when they persecute you in this city, flee ye into another:"

However, when they afflict (persecute) you in your presence, leave them peacefully going unto another willing to listen to the good news of the gospels.

Comment appropriately to "for verily I say unto you, Ye shall not have gone over the cities of Israel, till the Son of man be come."

For indeed, I give my disciples insights on how to enter God's Kingdom. Certainly, those presently near the kingdom of heaven shall find rest. Furthermore, you will unfold the fullness of life when the Son of man has been revealed in the second coming.

KJV Matthew 10: verse 24

The disciple is not above *his* master, nor the servant above his lord.

Comment appropriately to "The disciple is not above *his* master, nor the servant above his lord."

Therefore, the sheep is not above the Shepard (master), nor is the angel above his God (lord).

KJV Matthew 10: verse 25

It is enough for the disciple that he be as his master, and the servant as his lord. If they have called the master of the house Beelzebub, how much more *shall they call* them of his household?

Comment appropriately to "It is enough for the disciple that he be as his master, and the servant as his lord."

Therefore, it is proper for disciples of Jesus Christ to live in their Savior's likeness and serve in the manner to all as one.

Comment appropriately to "If they have called the master of the house Beelzebub, how much more *shall they call* them of his household?"

Thus, if he is the master of the soul's subconscious mind disciplined from evil (Beelzebub), how much more significant is the consciousness inwardly?

KJV Matthew 10: verse 26

Fear them not therefore: for there is nothing covered, that shall not be revealed; and hid, that shall not be known.

Comment appropriately to "Fear them not therefore: for there is nothing covered, that shall not be revealed;"

For this reason, do not fear them at all! For all things that are covered shall be uncovered. In the same way, all righteous thoughts will reveal truths.

Comment appropriately to "and hid, that shall not be known."

That which is in darkness shall remain hidden by my commandments.

KJV Matthew 10: verse 27

What I tell you in darkness, *that* speak ye in light: and what ye hear in the ear, *that* preach ye upon the housetops.

Comment appropriately to "What I tell you in darkness, *that* speak ye in light:"

Teach others what I have shared with you in solitude. More importantly, do not fear any man because of what you have received from me. Do this freely speaking to all.

Comment appropriately to "and what ye hear in the ear, *that* preach ye upon the housetops."

While in mindfulness of one, you have heard in seclusion. Thus, be compelled to give moral teachings for those seeking truths to enter the kingdom of heaven.

KJV Matthew 10: verse 28

And fear not them which kill the body, but are not able to kill the soul: but rather fear him which is able to destroy both soul and body in hell.

Comment appropriately to "And fear not them which kill the body, but are not able to kill the soul:"

Likewise, do not fear those who live in the divided subconscious mind unaware of their true nature. Yet, they are unable to harm their spirit.

Comment appropriately to "but rather fear him which is able to destroy both soul and body in hell."

Similarly, despair those souls that consume the spirit and subconscious mind to both lies and vain repetition.

KJV Matthew 10: verse 29

Are not two sparrows sold for a farthing? and one of them shall not fall on the ground without your Father.

Comment appropriately to "Are not two sparrows sold for a farthing? and one of them shall not fall on the ground without your Father."

Indeed, are you more valuable than thoughts and emotions (two sparrows) within the heart where the Father dwells? Therefore, your unseen Father in heaven has a shield of everlasting Love for you.

KJV Matthew 10: verse 30

But the very hairs of your head are all numbered.

Comment appropriately to "But the very hairs of your head are all numbered."

Indeed, as thy days are numbered here in this foreign land (earthly plain), be passers-by.

KJV Matthew 10: verse 31

Fear ye not therefore, ye are of more value than many sparrows.

Comment appropriately to "Fear ye not therefore, ye are of more value than many sparrows."

Therefore, fear not because you are more valuable than you can ever imagine (sparrows) for thy wealth in heaven.

KJV Matthew 10: verse 32

Whosoever therefore shall confess me before men, him will I confess also before my Father which is in heaven.

Comment appropriately to "Whosoever therefore shall confess me before men, him will I confess also before my

Father which is in heaven."

Indeed, whoever confesses before evil doers (men) within their heart that Jesus Christ is Lord. So shall I certainly receive you likewise before my Father which art in consciousness (heaven).

KJV Matthew 10: verse 33

But whosoever shall deny me before men, him will I also deny before my Father which is in heaven.

Comment appropriately to "But whosoever shall deny me before men, him will I also deny before my Father which is in heaven."

Likewise, whoever denies me within their heart before evil doers (men), the Lord most certainly will deny you before the Father which art in heaven.

KJV Matthew 10: verse 34

Think not that I am come to send peace on earth: I came not to send peace, but a sword.

Comment appropriately to "Think not that I am come to send peace on earth: I came not to send peace, but a sword."

Without doubt, I have come upon the earth plain not to restore peace and calm. On the contrary, my purpose is to spread pure truth (sword) from the word of God in my new commandments.

KJV Matthew 10: verse 35

For I am come to set a man at variance against his father, and the daughter against her mother, and the daughter in law against her mother in law.

Comment appropriately to "For I am come to set a man at variance against his father,"

Thus, I have come to conclude conflict within the subconscious mind between the Self, righteousness -and the Father of the alter-ego opposing the Father's will.

Comment appropriately to "and the daughter against her mother,"

In truth, the daughter refers to the mind or domain of the Self. Hence, a soul is male, and the reason is female. Thus, when referring to the mother, it references the Father's mind or Kingdom in Heaven.

Comment appropriately to "and the daughter in law against her mother in law."

Nonetheless, in this case, the daughter-in-law and her mother-in-law belong rightfully to the spiritually dead those not awoken.

KJV Matthew 10: verse 36

And a man's foes *shall be* they of his own household.

Comment appropriately to "And a man's foes *shall be* they of his own household."

Thus, a man's mind, or shall we say divided mind. Hence, he will remain in his domain upon denying the teachings of Christ our Lord.

KJV Matthew 10: verse 37

He that loveth father or mother more than me is not worthy of me: and he that loveth son or daughter more than me is not worthy of me.

Comment appropriately to "He that loveth father or mother more than me is not worthy of me:"

Therefore, if he loves his earthly mother or earthly dad more than me, then you are not worthy of my everlasting devotion, for I am thy Lord God on high!

Comment appropriately to "and he that loveth son or daughter more than me is not worthy of me."

Furthermore, he that loves a son or daughter more than me is also not worthy of my everlasting devotion, for I am thy Lord God on high!

KJV Matthew 10: verse 38

And he that taketh not his cross, and followeth after me, is not worthy of me.

Comment appropriately to "And he that taketh not his cross, and followeth after me, is not worthy of me."

For this purpose, he that does not take up their *cross* (surrender to a high purpose) in the same manner as me and *follows me* (do not deviate from the teachings of Christ). You are not worthy of my unyielding devotion.

Note: Jesus is conveying to his disciples on reasoning and attitudes for entering the kingdom. In this understanding, he is a jealous God and by Love. Should be first in all things.

KJV Matthew 10: verse 39

He that findeth his life shall lose it: and he that loseth his life for my sake shall find it.

Comment appropriately to "He that findeth his life shall lose it: and he that loseth his life for my sake shall find it."

In this parable, Jesus is directing the elect on how to proceed in finding the kingdom. Thus, to see life is like finding purpose; however, you must surrender to a high calling or purpose. To find a human life is lost against its soul.

In addition, to lose your life for Christ's sake is to lose your life to discover purity of Love. You lose your life for all be that it may, or whatever may or may not happen.

Love is the key and life's blood.

KJV Matthew 10: verse 40

He that receiveth you receiveth me, and he that receiveth me receiveth him that sent me.

Comment appropriately to "He that receiveth you receiveth me, and he that receiveth me receiveth him that sent me."

The Father received you as he has received me the Son, and he the Father has accepted you also, have indeed received me.

KJV Matthew 10: verse 41

He that receiveth a prophet in the name of a prophet shall receive a prophet's reward; and he that receiveth a righteous man in the name of a righteous man shall receive a righteous man's reward.

Comment appropriately to "He that receiveth a prophet in the name of a prophet shall receive a prophet's reward;"

The deceiver does not know God's will in my name and shall indeed receive a deceiver's reward, thus living in a divided mind.

Comment appropriately to "and he that receiveth a righteous man in the name of a righteous man shall receive a righteous man's reward."

Also, the righteous man shall bestow in my name honest thoughts and ideas leading to the treasures in heaven. Indeed, the Father takes pleasure in giving moral rewards.

KJV Matthew 10: verse 42

And whosoever shall give to drink unto one of these little ones a cup of cold *water* only in the name of a disciple, verily I say unto you, he shall in no wise lose his reward.

Comment appropriately to "And whosoever shall give to drink unto one of these little ones a cup of cold *water* only in the name of a disciple,"

Therefore, whoever gives you a cup of Love (drink) life (water) unto one of these children a cup quenches their thirst only in my name Jesus Christ.

Comment appropriately to "verily I say unto you, he shall in no wise lose his reward."

Indeed, I honestly tell you that he will in no way lose any Love or his accolade in the kingdom of heaven.

Matthew Chapter 11

KJV Matthew 11: verse 4

Jesus answered and said unto them, Go and shew John again those things which ye do hear and see:

Comment appropriately to "Go and shew John again those things which ye do hear and see:"

Go unto John the Baptist and shed light on those things he prophesied in truth from heaven. Hence, the lamb of God who restores man's faith is indeed the Messiah that John the Baptist told you in the wilderness.

These revelations are in truthfulness before all nations (souls).

KJV Matthew 11: verse 5

The blind receive their sight, and the lame walk, the lepers are cleansed, and the deaf hear, the dead are raised up, and the poor have the gospel preached to them.

Comment appropriately to "The blind receive their sight, and the lame walk, the lepers are cleansed, and the deaf hear, the dead are raised up,"

In truth, the spiritually sleep (blind) and the other in the human body have their sight. The weary spirit walks by faith as too the physical body.

The blemishes of untruths on the subconscious mind, and the skin cleansed because its hearth their Shepherd's voice.

Thus, the souls hearing the vibrational particles for hearing. So, indeed, the righteous in spirit have been made whole in the rising as too the physical body.

Comment appropriately to "and the poor have the gospel preached to them."

Forever, the poor (fearful, jealous, anxiety, anger, envious, doubtful etc.) in spirit have the New Commandment in my New Testaments given unto them.

KJV Matthew 11: verse 6

And blessed is *he*, whosoever shall not be offended in me.

Comment appropriately to "And blessed is *he*, whosoever shall not be offended in me"

Blessed is those (Sheep) who glorify my truths within their subconscious mind.

KJV Matthew 11: verse 7

And as they departed, Jesus began to say unto the multitudes concerning John, What went ye out into the wilderness to see? A reed shaken with the wind?

Comment appropriately to "What went ye out into the wilderness to see? A reed shaken with the wind?"

Therefore, what did you seek after in your subconscious mind that holds all truths? Nonetheless, your spirit is in the spiritual winds (reed shaken) of this physical world.

KJV Matthew 11: verse 8

But what went ye out for to see? A man clothed in soft raiment? behold, they that wear soft *clothing* are in kings' houses.

Comment appropriately to "But what went ye out for to see? A man clothed in soft raiment?"

Nevertheless, what did you find in your subconscious mind? Is a spirit searching for the reasoning behind unrighteous thoughts or guilt (soft raiment) held in the subconscious mind?

Comment appropriately to "behold, they that wear soft *clothing* are in kings' houses."

Observe, those who wear condemnation or guilt (soft clothing) in their divided mind hurt their souls (kings' houses).

KJV Matthew 11: verse 9

But what went ye out for to see? A prophet? yea, I say unto you, and more than a prophet.

Comment appropriately to "But what went ye out for to see? A prophet? yea, I say unto you, and more than a prophet."

Again, what did you find in your subconscious mind? A teacher of spiritual truths? Yes, **(I am)** truthfully more than a teacher or prophet. **I am thy Lord, thy God.**

KJV Matthew 11: verse 10

For this is *he*, of whom it is written, Behold, I send my messenger before thy face, which shall prepare thy way before thee.

Comment appropriately to "For this is *he*, of whom it is written, Behold, I send my messenger before thy face, which shall prepare thy way before thee."

For it is the Christ (the Messiah) of whom written in the First Testament. Before, it was prophesied concerning a messenger to come before him and alert those walking in darkness.

KJV Matthew 11: verse 11

Verily I say unto you, Among them that are born of women there hath not risen a greater than John the Baptist: notwithstanding he that is least in the kingdom of heaven is greater than he.

Comment appropriately to "Verily I say unto you, Among them that are born of women there hath not risen a greater than John the Baptist:"

Truly I say this on entering the Kingdom of God, of all children born on earth of a woman in physical form. None have been more significant in spiritual awareness than John the Baptist.

Comment appropriately to "notwithstanding he that is least in the kingdom of heaven is greater than he."

Nevertheless, John the Baptist did not know himself to be a spiritual being holding all truths of those to enter the kingdom of heaven. In which those who do enter the Kingdom of God will be higher in spiritual revelations.

KJV Matthew 11: verse 12

And from the days of John the Baptist until now the kingdom of heaven suffereth violence, and the violent take it by force.

Comment appropriately to "And from the days of John the Baptist until now the kingdom of heaven suffereth violence, and the violent take it by force."

The scriptures suffered disorder with the many edits of evildoers for earthly gains in dividing the church into denominations until John the Baptist.

KJV Matthew 11: verse 13

For all the prophets and the law prophesied until John.

Comment appropriately to "For all the prophets and the law prophesied until John."

Thus, authoritarian spiritual truth and teachers of the law

warned you even before John the Baptist.

KJV Matthew 11: verse 14

And if ye will receive *it*, this is Elias, which was for to come.

Comment appropriately to "And if ye will receive *it*, this is Elias, which was for to come."

If you accept this truth in your spirit, he "Elias" was reincarnated before you now.

Note: Let's discern this notion of reincarnations right here, right now! Jesus, the Messiah, in spirit could not under any circumstance form lies by virtue. Being conscious means being full of truths. In layman's terms, "He ***was perfect in everyway***!"

Again, this is true "only" if you are willing to accept that we do indeed come back to reincarnate in the physical.

KJV Matthew 11: verse 15

He that hath ears to hear, let him hear.

Comment appropriately to "He that hath cars to hear, let him hear."

He is capable of understanding and accepting these truths (state of mind). Let him receive (hear).

KJV Matthew 11: verse 16

But whereunto shall I liken this generation? It is like unto children sitting in the markets, and calling unto their fellows,

Comment appropriately to "But whereunto shall I liken this generation?"

However, who shall I call before the kingdom of heaven in these repugnance times?

Comment appropriately to "It is like unto children sitting in the markets, and calling unto their fellows,"

Although, it is like a child searching for truths in the subconscious mind while searching in the synagogues (markets).

KJV Matthew 11: verse 17

And saying, We have piped unto you, and ye have not danced; we have mourned unto you, and ye have not lamented.

Comment appropriately to "And saying, We have piped unto you, and ye have not danced; we have mourned unto you, and ye have not lamented."

Thus, claiming we have called out for righteous thinking, and you do not provide it; we have suffered waiting for your honest thoughts, and yet you have deceived us from your divided mind.

KJV Matthew 11: verse 18

For John came neither eating nor drinking, and they say, He hath a devil.

Comment appropriately to "For John came neither eating

nor drinking, and they say, He hath a devil."

Yet, John the Baptist came with pure intentions of clearing a way for the Messiah. Choosing to eat what was natural from the earth, not drinking alcohol, and thus you say, he was wicked in mind.

KJV Matthew 11: verse 19

The Son of man came eating and drinking, and they say, Behold a man gluttonous, and a winebibber, a friend of publicans and sinners. But wisdom is justified of her children.

Comment appropriately to "The Son of man came eating and drinking, and they say, Behold a man gluttonous, and a winebibber, a friend of publicans and sinners."

In faith, the Son of the Father comes in righteousness, celebrating eating with evildoers while drinking wines with Love. Yet, despite this, you say he is a ravenous, drunkenness to wine, companion to the unrighteous trespassers.

Comment appropriately to "But wisdom is justified of her children."

However, with all her wisdom, she justifies a child of God.

Note: Be that is may, and if you are willing to accept. There is a spirit of God's wisdom in spiritual form and in full consciousness of itself.

KJV Matthew 11: verse 21

Woe unto thee, Chorazin! woe unto thee, Bethsaida! for if

the mighty works, which were done in you, had been done in Tyre and Sidon, they would have repented long ago in sackcloth and ashes.

Comment appropriately to "Woe unto thee, Chorazin! woe unto thee, Bethsaida! for if the mighty works, which were done in you, had been done in Tyre and Sidon,"

Moreover, afflictions to Chorazin and suffering Bethsaida! Considering the miracle that I did in your presence had been done likewise to "Tyre and Sidon."

Comment appropriately to "they would have repented long ago in sackcloth and ashes."

Thus, these believers of Christ (presence of miracle) would have confessed unrighteous thoughts and guilt (sackcloth) held in the subconscious mind with tears (ashes).

KJV Matthew 11: verse 22

But I say unto you, It shall be more tolerable for Tyre and Sidon at the day of judgment, than for you.

Comment appropriately to "But I say unto you, It shall be more tolerable for Tyre and Sidon at the day of judgment, than for you."

Therefore, in my new commandments, Tyre and Sidon shall have more mercy (tolerance) than you in the end of days.

KJV Matthew 11: verse 23

And thou, Capernaum, which art exalted unto heaven, shalt

be brought down to hell: for if the mighty works, which have been done in thee, had been done in Sodom, it would have remained until this day.

Comment appropriately to "And thou, Capernaum, which art exalted unto heaven, shalt be brought down to hell: for if the mighty works, which have been done in thee,"

Although, in the presence (city of Capernaum), which is honored in consciousness. In principle had been destroyed by evildoers' (hells-fire) in the subconscious mind.

However, had the cleansing of your energy centers (mighty works) been done in you.

Comment appropriately to "had been done in Sodom, it would have remained until this day."

Thus, these mighty works had been in the divided mind (Sodom); it (the results) would have remained until this very day.

KJV Matthew 11: verse 24

But I say unto you, That it shall be more tolerable for the land of Sodom in the day of judgment, than for thee.

Comment appropriately to "But I say unto you,"

Jesus again is making us aware of how to enter God's Kingdom.

Comment appropriately to "That it shall be more tolerable for the land of Sodom in the day of judgment, than for thee."

Take repentance because living in the divided mind (Sodom) is therefore remaining unrighteous is more forgivable for you.

KJV Matthew 11: verse 25

At that time Jesus answered and said, I thank thee, O Father, Lord of heaven and earth, because thou hast hid these things from the wise and prudent, and hast revealed them unto babes.

Comment appropriately to "I thank thee, O Father, Lord of heaven and earth, because thou hast hid these things from the wise"

Graciously, I thank you, Heavenly Father, for thee are rulers over heaven and earth, and you have hidden my teachings from teachers of the law of Moses in the First Testament.

Comment appropriately to "and prudent, and hast revealed them unto babes."

In your compassion, have revealed in secrecy to your children seeking Love and truth.

KJV Matthew 11: verse 26

Even so, Father: for so it seemed good in thy sight.

Comment appropriately to "Even so, Father: for so it seemed good in thy sight."

Indeed, Father, all things are good before your sight.

KJV Matthew 11: verse 27

All things are delivered unto me of my Father: and no man knoweth the Son, but the Father; neither knoweth any man the Father, save the Son, and *he* to whomsoever the Son will reveal *him*.

Comment appropriately to "All things are delivered unto me of my Father: and no man knoweth the Son, but the Father; neither knoweth any man the Father, save the Son,"

Indeed, all things given to me are from the Father. However, no man knows me as the Son but the Father; likewise, no man has seen the Father, only the Son the Messiah.

Comment appropriately to "and *he* to whomsoever the Son will reveal *him*."

And the Father, who indeed reveals unto him the Son of the Living Father.

KJV Matthew 11: verse 28

Come unto me, all *ye* that labour and are heavy laden, and I will give you rest.

Comment appropriately to "Come unto me, all *ye* that labour and are heavy laden, and I will give you rest."

Therefore, come to me my sheep who doeth the Father's work and are fatigued from this world as I will give you comfort.

KJV Matthew 11: verse 29

Take my yoke upon you, and learn of me; for I am meek and lowly in heart: and ye shall find rest unto your souls.

Comment appropriately to "Take my yoke upon you, and learn of me; for I am meek and lowly in heart:"

With this purpose in mind, lay your unrighteous thoughts on me, learn from my teachings. Thy Lord is gentle and full of Love in the heart.

Comment appropriately to "and ye shall find rest unto your souls."

For you will find peace and rest within your mind and spiritual body.

KJV Matthew 11: verse 30

For my yoke *is* easy, and my burden is light.

Comment appropriately to "For my yoke *is* easy, and my burden is light."

Indeed, my righteous thoughts are uncomplicated, and my concerns are unimportant.

Matthew Chapter 12

KJV Matthew 12: verse 3

But he said unto them, Have ye not read what David did, when he was an hungred, and they that were with him;

Comment appropriately to "Have ye not read what David did, when he was an hungred, and they that were with him;"

As we begin with this parable, our Lord Jesus is bringing awareness to the Sadducees on how they are unwilling to acknowledge the existence of the coming Messiah. In addition, the obligation to their oral tradition.

In this passage, did you avoid reading in the First/Old Testament what David did once he entered the temple? Additionally, what did he and others do in the synagogue?

Note: Conversely, Jesus was making the priest realize their laws were meaningless because they only served the Sadducees and not the children of God.

KJV Matthew 12: verse 4

How he entered into the house of God, and did eat the

shewbread, which was not lawful for him to eat, neither for them which were with him, but only for the priests?

Comment appropriately to "How he entered into the house of God, and did eat the shewbread, which was not lawful for him to eat, neither for them which were with him, but only for the priests?"

Despite it being the house of Prayer, he did indeed partake of the leaven, which was forbidden to eat with others that were with him according to scripture and laws written by unrighteous holy men!

Note: Again, the Messiah is making it very precise and clear how not only did David disobey their law so quickly. Others did as well because of its unrighteous thinking.

KJV Matthew 12: verse 5

Or have ye not read in the law, how that on the sabbath days the priests in the temple profane the sabbath, and are blameless?

Comment appropriately to "Or have ye not read in the law, how that on the sabbath days the priests in the temple profane the sabbath, and are blameless?"

Notwithstanding, are the rules written by holy men of God. They edit the laws in favor of the priest in the tabernacles. Thus, they did not observe the Lord's Day of rest (sabbath) from the world and remaining from criticism because of their evil deeds and thoughts (blameless).

KJV Matthew 12: verse 6

But I say unto you, That in this place is *one* greater than the temple.

Comment appropriately to "But I say unto you, That in this place is *one* greater than the temple."

However, in the kingdom of heaven, there is a consciousness (one greater) more harmonious than any house of Worship.

KJV Matthew 12: verse 7

But if ye had known what *this* meaneth, I will have mercy, and not sacrifice, ye would not have condemned the guiltless.

Comment appropriately to "But if ye had known what *this* meaneth, I will have mercy, and not sacrifice, ye would not have condemned the guiltless"

However, if you truly understood my words in spirit, I come to give compassion (mercy) and not atonement (not sacrifice) because you have judged the innocent souls (guiltless).

KJV Matthew 12: verse 8

For the Son of man is Lord even of the sabbath day.

Comment appropriately to "For the Son of man is Lord even of the sabbath day."

Indeed, the Savior Jesus Christ is Lord God, even on the day of rest (sabbath) from the world.

KJV Matthew 12: verse 11

And he said unto them, What man shall there be among you, that shall have one sheep, and if it fall into a pit on the sabbath day, will he not lay hold on it, and lift *it* out?

Comment appropriately to "And he said unto them, What man shall there be among you, that shall have one sheep, and if it fall into a pit on the sabbath day, will he not lay hold on it, and lift *it* out?"

In this parable, Jesus is bringing light into his new commandments.

Thus, what Shepard amongst any of you would allow one sheep (Follower of Christ) to go astray (fall in the pit) on the day our Lord (sabbath) as set for rest? Hence, will not seek its comfort with Love?

KJV Matthew 12: verse 12

How much then is a man better than a sheep? Wherefore it is lawful to do well on the sabbath days.

Comment appropriately to "How much then is a man better than a sheep? Wherefore it is lawful to do well on the sabbath days."

If the sheep go missing, how worthy is this Shepard, thus allowing Love to be distant from the herd? Indeed, this is permissible to seek on the day of rest (sabbath).

Note: Sheep are souls who have accepted Jesus Christ as one with God in Trinity, Lord, Savior, and the Messiah. Those able to understand and desire truths from the teachings of the New Testament.

KJV Matthew 12: verse 13

Then saith he to the man, Stretch forth thine hand. And he stretched *it* forth; and it was restored whole, like as the other.

Comment appropriately to "Stretch forth thine hand."

Understanding how our Lord is of consciousness in the spiritual body refers to the heart (hand). Thus, in Love for the healing, "Expand forward thy heart" for truths within.

KJV Matthew 12: verse 25

And Jesus knew their thoughts, and said unto them, Every kingdom divided against itself is brought to desolation; and every city or house divided against itself shall not stand:

Comment appropriately to "Every kingdom divided against itself is brought to desolation;"

In man's mind, which divides in the subconscious (alter-ego), it cannot stand against one another because it's devastation good versus evil.

Comment appropriately to "and every city or house divided against itself shall not stand:"

Therefore, every soul (house) or men's mind is divided against itself will not stand (no inner peace).

KJV Matthew 12: verse 26

And if Satan cast out Satan, he is divided against himself; how shall then his kingdom stand?

Comment appropriately to "And if Satan cast out Satan, he is divided against himself; how shall then his kingdom stand?"

So, if a divided mind portrays good and evil (Satan) is divided against itself. Then, how will the power stand together?

Note: Satan is used as a metaphor to describe and characterize man's mind - hence the alter-ego (human mind).

KJV Matthew 12: verse 27

And if I by Beelzebub cast out devils, by whom do your children cast *them* out? therefore they shall be your judges.

Comment appropriately to "And if I by Beelzebub cast out devils, by whom do your children cast *them* out?"

Moreover, if these demon minds (Beelzebub) decide to cast out the same demon-like thoughts in the same manner.

So then, how will or to whom will your worshipers (children) of the Law/Old Testament find peace in their subconscious?

Comment appropriately to "therefore they shall be your judges."

For this reason, your churchgoers (judges) will not find

God's Kingdom and in no way find peace in renewing their mind under false doctrine.

KJV Matthew 12: verse 28

But if I cast out devils by the Spirit of God, then the kingdom of God is come unto you.

Comment appropriately to "But if I cast out devils by the Spirit of God, then the kingdom of God is come unto you."

However, if Thy Lord Jesus Christ does banish out evil thoughts by the Father's Holy Spirit, then indeed, the kingdom of God is present with you always.

KJV Matthew 12: verse 29

Or else how can one enter into a strong man's house, and spoil his goods, except he first bind the strong man? and then he will spoil his house.

Comment appropriately to "Or else how can one enter into a strong man's house, and spoil his goods, except he first bind the strong man?"

Therefore, by faith and knowledge of the kingdom of God, how can you challenge a believer's (strong man) soul (house) concerning the teachings of Jesus Christ in the New Testament?

Notwithstanding, impair (spoil) his belief of true worship on transcendental meditation (goods) unless you impose old scripture (bind) on the believer (strong man) against the New Commandments?

Comment appropriately to "and then he will spoil his house."

Then, and only then, will you have a chance to corrupt his soul (house)?

KJV Matthew 12: verse 30

He that is not with me is against me; and he that gathereth not with me scattereth abroad.

Comment appropriately to "He that is not with me is against me; and he that gathereth not with me scattereth abroad."

Therefore, he who does not accept my New Commandments is indeed opposed to entering the Kingdom of God; thus, he that does not come unto me and believeth in my way of worship.

He shall indeed remain outside of the consciousness of heaven.

KJV Matthew 12: verse 31

Wherefore I say unto you, All manner of sin and blasphemy shall be forgiven unto men: but the blasphemy *against* the *Holy* Ghost shall not be forgiven unto men.

Comment appropriately to "Wherefore I say unto you, All manner of sin and blasphemy shall be forgiven unto men:"

Jesus is bringing awareness of his New Commandments on Love and Truth.

Thus, our Lord is clarifying, our Lord God shall forgive every misdeed, transgression, wrongdoing made before our Father in heaven.

Comment appropriately to "but the blasphemy *against* the *Holy* Ghost shall not be forgiven unto men."

However, under no circumstance will blaspheming against God's Love (Holy Spirit) for any reason **will not** be forgiven.

Note: To come against God's Holy Spirit is very unacceptable and has severe consequences. Essentially, you are challenging our Father's genuine Love for each of us.

(DO NOT DO THIS AT ALL, AND FOR ANY REASON).

For God is Love. (Enough Said).

KJV Matthew 12: verse 32

And whosoever speaketh a word against the Son of man, it shall be forgiven him: but whosoever speaketh against the Holy Ghost, it shall not be forgiven him, neither in this world, neither in the *world* to come.

Comment appropriately to "And whosoever speaketh a word against the Son of man, it shall be forgiven him:"

Likewise, those opposing our Lord and Savior and because of Love and truth; are forgiven as well.

Comment appropriately to "whosoever speaketh against the Holy Ghost, it shall not be forgiven him, neither in this world, neither in the *world* to come."

However, again and under no circumstance will blaspheming against God's Love (Holy Spirit) for any reason **will not** be forgiven upon earth or any other dimension.

KJV Matthew 12: verse 33

Either make the tree good, and his fruit good; or else make the tree corrupt, and his fruit corrupt: for the tree is known by *his* fruit.

Comment appropriately to "Either make the tree good, and his fruit good; or else make the tree corrupt, and his fruit corrupt:"

Furthermore, make the appointed soul worthy of truths (tree) from the heart, and his *knowledge and understanding* (good fruit) will fuel the spiritual body.

On the other hand, make the alter ego (human mind) untruths, and he will bring forth unrighteousness from the heart.

Comment appropriately to "for the tree is known by *his* fruit."

Likewise, you will recognize their heart in their demeanor by their knowledge of spirit.

KJV Matthew 12: verse 34

O generation of vipers, how can ye, being evil, speak good things? for out of the abundance of the heart the mouth speaketh.

Comment appropriately to "O generation of vipers, how can ye, being evil, speak good things? for out of the abundance of the heart the mouth speaketh."

Oh, you are a reproduction of evil thoughts (vipers) who say such hurtful things to others? How dare you bring forth much anger by speaking such corrupt words?

How do you intend to find Love in your speech if you do not follow my teachings? Indeed, what plethora of displeasure you speak comes from within the heart.

KJV Matthew 12: verse 35

A good man out of the good treasure of the heart bringeth forth good things: and an evil man out of the evil treasure bringeth forth evil things.

Comment appropriately to "A good man out of the good treasure of the heart bringeth forth good things:"

A true believer of Jesus Christ and his teachings brings forth righteousness (treasure) in speech because he speaks truthfully from the heart.

Comment appropriately to "and an evil man out of the evil treasure bringeth forth evil things."

An evildoer knows not the heart's inner workings because he denies the Christ within and the teachings. Thus, evil works and speech come from his heart.

KJV Matthew 12: verse 36

But I say unto you, That every idle word that men shall speak, they shall give account thereof in the day of judgment.

Comment appropriately to "But I say unto you, That every idle word that men shall speak, they shall give account thereof in the day of judgment."

Our Lord Jesus is making us aware of understanding his New Commandments. Thus, with every reflection (idle word); hence, our inner thoughts, which become our speech, will be confronted by the *Universal Law of Cause and Effect* (judgment). Even at the end of time (physical death).

KJV Matthew 12: verse 37

For by thy words thou shalt be justified, and by thy words thou shalt be condemned.

Comment appropriately to "For by thy words thou shalt be justified, and by thy words thou shalt be condemned."

In other words, what you put out into the Universal by thoughts or speech mixed with emotions (justified), shall indeed bring forth and manifest (condemn) you in ways of teaching a better way to Love.

KJV Matthew 12: verse 39

But he answered and said unto them, An evil and adulterous generation seeketh after a sign; and there shall no sign be given to it, but the sign of the prophet Jonas:

Comment appropriately to "But he answered and said unto them, An evil and adulterous generation seeketh after a sign;"

Thus, Jesus spoke concerning his new commandments to the spiritually dead; saying, those who keep unrighteous thoughts in this society always desire proof of its guilt of adulterous lust.

Comment appropriately to "and there shall no sign be given to it, but the sign of the prophet Jonas:"

Therefore, in the evilness of your adulterous desires, you shall in no way receive a sign other than proof of the prophet Jonas.

KJV Matthew 12: verse 40

For as Jonas was three days and three nights in the whale's belly; so shall the Son of man be three days and three nights in the heart of the earth.

Comment appropriately to "For as Jonas was three days and three nights in the whale's belly;"

Indeed, of witness testimony, Jonas spent three days and three nights in the belly of a large mammal.

Comment appropriately to "so shall the Son of man be three days and three nights in the heart of the earth."

In the same way, the Son of man (the Messiah) will indeed spend three days and nights in the heart (spiritual body of the Self), therefore consciousness with creation.

In truth, the evolution of a soul's desire for completion proceeds in the full consciousness of an awakening.

In the same way, the cycles of desires take on three parts of the manifest: thus, evening, night, and morning - finalizing Self's desire hence, Day (completion).

KJV Matthew 12: verse 41

The men of Nineveh shall rise in judgment with this generation, and shall condemn it: because they repented at the preaching of Jonas; and, behold, a greater than Jonas *is* here.

Comment appropriately to "The men of Nineveh shall rise in judgment with this generation, and shall condemn it: because they repented at the preaching of Jonas;"

Consequently, Jonas warned the men of Nineveh who repented and obtained God's mercy will exceed this society because they will be found guilty in their adulterous ways.

Comment appropriately to "and, behold, a greater than Jonas *is* here."

Indeed, before Jonas was, and in the presence of your spirit, God's Son is present in the now.

KJV Matthew 12: verse 42

The queen of the south shall rise up in the judgment with this generation, and shall condemn it: for she came from the uttermost parts of the earth to hear the wisdom of Solomon; and, behold, a greater than Solomon *is* here.

Comment appropriately to "The queen of the south shall rise up in the judgment with this generation, and shall condemn it:"

In particular, the Queen of Sheba, a beautiful African queen referred to as the queen of the south, found much wisdom in Solomon.

Thus, she found spiritual truths and would have also condemn this society of its adulterous ways.

Comment appropriately to "for she came from the uttermost parts of the earth to hear the wisdom of Solomon;"

Granted that, she went to great lengths to search for answers that were already within herself (consciousness) of the prophet Solomon.

Comment appropriately to "and, behold, a greater than Solomon *is* here."

Yet in still, and before Solomon was, in all its glory transcendent of spirit (the Messiah) and God's Kingdom is here.

KJV Matthew 12: verse 43

When the unclean spirit is gone out of a man, he walketh through dry places, seeking rest, and findeth none.

Comment appropriately to "When the unclean spirit is gone out of a man, he walketh through dry places, seeking rest, and findeth none."

Accordingly, when an unrighteous soul's subconscious (human mind) of the alter ego believes in its righteousness (dry places), it looks for a feeling of peace (rest) within itself and finds none.

KJV Matthew 12: verse 44

Then he saith, I will return into my house from whence I came out; and when he is come, he findeth *it* empty, swept, and garnished.

Comment appropriately to "Then he saith, I will return into my house from whence I came out;"

As a result, the soul (house) decides to return within himself (subconscious mind) from where he momentarily vacated.

Comment appropriately to "and when he is come, he findeth *it* empty, swept, and garnished."

However, when he regathered conscious thought of his alter ego (human mind), he found it with untruths (empty), lies of happiness in material substance or earthly riches (swept), and filled with unrighteous fruit (garnished).

KJV Matthew 12: verse 45

Then goeth he, and taketh with himself seven other spirits more wicked than himself, and they enter in and dwell there: and the last *state* of that man is worse than the first. Even so shall it be also unto this wicked generation.

Comment appropriately to "Then goeth he, and taketh with himself seven other spirits more wicked than himself, and they enter in and dwell there:"

Despite this aggression within the consciousness of the mind, the soul seeks refuge outside of himself (gathers more material substance), obtaining seven more spirits more wicked than himself. Notwithstanding, they come to dwell within him.

Note: While in this parable, our Lord is illustrating a state of being within the mind of those chasing earthly riches before the realization of the Self (God within).

Be it that it may, the seven spirits that come within one's consciousness are to remind us of works necessary to gain conscious awareness. In other words, for us to discover our identity.

Those seven spirits include the **Spirit of the Lord**, and the **Spirits of Wisdom** (Lady Wisdom), **Spirit of Understanding** (Winds of Influence), of **Counsel** (Ascended Guides), **God's Might** (Power of God), **Spirit of Knowledge** (Christ Jesus the Bread Keeper), and lastly, the **Fear of the LORD**.

Comment appropriately to "and the last *state* of that man is worse than the first. Even so shall it be also unto this wicked generation."

Indeed, the state of mind is worse than initially obtained upon reincarnation into a new physical body. But, at the end of the day (physical death), this is how it will be with this society.

KJV Matthew 12: verse 48

But he answered and said unto him that told him, Who is my mother? and who are my brethren?

Comment appropriately to "Who is my mother? and who are my brethren?"

Truly indeed, who is my mother? Likewise, who are my brothers?

Note: In truth, Jesus is making us aware of how things indeed are in the kingdom of heaven.

We are of one consciousness, and by this, heaven is our mother; thus, we all are brothers and sisters when Love exists.

KJV Matthew 12: verse 49

And he stretched forth his hand toward his disciples, and said, Behold my mother and my brethren!

Comment appropriately to "Behold my mother and my brethren!"

For this reasoning and understanding, when Love does exist in consciousness, here is my mother, and here are my brethren.

KJV Matthew 12: verse 50

For whosoever shall do the will of my Father which is in heaven, the same is my brother, and sister, and mother.

Comment appropriately to "For whosoever shall do the

will of my Father which is in heaven,"

So, those soul's willing to do the will (Love) of the Father in heaven.

Comment appropriately to "the same is my brother, and sister, and mother."

All will share a genuine love for one another in my brother, sister, and my mother.

Matthew Chapter 13

KJV Matthew 13: verse 3

And he spake many things unto them in parables, saying, Behold, a sower went forth to sow;

Comment appropriately to "Behold, a sower went forth to sow;"

Meanwhile, a farmer (one who is authorized to instruct the New Teachings) went out into the world to share (sow) the great news of the gospels of Christ.

KJV Matthew 13: verse 4

And when he sowed, some *seeds* fell by the way side, and the fowls came and devoured them up:

Comment appropriately to "And when he sowed, some *seeds* fell by the way side, and the fowls came and devoured them up:"

Thus, he shared the great news of worshiping (seed) in Christ with observers, and the birds (deceitful thoughts in the subconscious mind) quickly wiped out those truths.

KJV Matthew 13: verse 5

Some fell upon stony places, where they had not much earth: and forthwith they sprung up, because they had no deepness of earth:

Comment appropriately to "Some fell upon stony places, where they had not much earth:"

Indeed, some fell on souls like a hurtful insult (stony) to their way of worship. Thus, they did not allow it to absorb into the subconscious mind (human mind).

Being spiritually blind, they dismissed the teachings altogether.

Comment appropriately to "and forthwith they sprung up, because they had no deepness of earth:"

Although the observers heard (sprung up) the new teachings in the gospels, these seeds did not take root in the subconscious mind (earth) because of the alter-ego mind.

KJV Matthew 13: verse 6

And when the sun was up, they were scorched; and because they had no root, they withered away.

Comment appropriately to "And when the sun was up, they were scorched; and because they had no root, they withered away."

Thus, when his faith in the teachings challenged the soul before others, he was ashamed (scorched) and quickly abandoned the instructions because he had little understanding (no root).

Hence, he shriveled up from righteous receiving of truths.

KJV Matthew 13: verse 7

And some fell among thorns; and the thorns sprung up, and choked them:

Comment appropriately to "And some fell among thorns; and the thorns sprung up, and choked them:"

Afterward, some seed fell on unrighteous thoughts (thorns); thus, wrongful thinking gathered in the subconscious mind and dismissed (choked) truths.

KJV Matthew 13: verse 8

But other fell into good ground, and brought forth fruit, some an hundredfold, some sixtyfold, some thirtyfold.

Comment appropriately to "But other fell into good ground, and brought forth fruit, some an hundredfold, some sixtyfold, some thirtyfold."

However, great news of the gospels of Christ fell on righteous thought (good ground) in the subconscious minds.

Most importantly, the teachings of Jesus Christ brought onwards one hundred times their value of Love, some sixty times their value, and even sometimes thirty times their value of understanding.

KJV Matthew 13: verse 9

Who hath ears to hear, let him hear.

Comment appropriately to "Who hath ears to hear, let him hear."

Those willing to accept these truths understand the spiritual secrets behind the teachings of Jesus Christ.

KJV Matthew 13: verse 11

He answered and said unto them, Because it is given unto you to know the mysteries of the kingdom of heaven, but to them it is not given.

Comment appropriately to "Because it is given unto you to know the mysteries of the kingdom of heaven, but to them it is not given."

Therefore, it has given consciousness in spirit my (Jesus) mysteries in secret to those who seek the kingdom of heaven. Not to those who are unwilling to do the works from the Father.

KJV Matthew 13: verse 12

For whosoever hath, to him shall be given, and he shall have more abundance: but whosoever hath not, from him shall be taken away even that he hath.

Comment appropriately to "For whosoever hath, to him shall be given, and he shall have more abundance:"

Above all, he that Loves all that is before him shall be given purely more abundantly.

Note: Initially, on the surface, you should consider the Universal Law of Manifestation. Then review this verse again in its entirety.

More uncomplicatedly put, you only get to keep what you give away and, in this case, purity of heart, hence Love!

Comment appropriately to "but whosoever hath not, from him shall be taken away even that he hath."

Consequently, he has little to no Love to share with others, and it too shall be lessened in the heart because he doesn't give it away to others.

Note: We are here to share Love in every form you can imagine.

KJV Matthew 13: verse 13

Therefore, speak I to them in parables: because they seeing see not; and hearing they hear not, neither do they understand.

Comment appropriately to "Therefore, speak I to them in parables: because they seeing see not; and hearing they hear not, neither do they understand."

Our Lord speaks to his disciples, stating that the spiritually blind do does not see spiritual truths (see with clarity).

Therefore, the spiritual soul denies spiritual hearing, nor does it accept spiritual ways (lack understanding).

KJV Matthew 13: verse 14

And in them is fulfilled the prophecy of Esaias, which saith, By hearing ye shall hear, and shall not understand; and seeing ye shall see, and shall not perceive:

Comment appropriately to "And in them is fulfilled the prophecy of Esaias, which saith, By hearing ye shall hear, and shall not understand; and seeing ye shall see, and shall not perceive:"

Thus, the prophet of Isaiah (Esaias) told of a Lord who came into the world. Still, a spiritual soul hears of Salvation, yet he does not understand; still seeing, however, not seeing all truths in higher understanding.

KJV Matthew 13: verse 15

For this people's heart is waxed gross, and *their* ears are dull of hearing, and their eyes they have closed; lest at any time they should see with *their* eyes, and hear with *their* ears, and should understand with *their* heart, and should be converted, and I should heal them.

Comment appropriately to "For this people's heart is waxed gross, and *their* ears are dull of hearing, and *their* eyes they have closed; lest at any time they should see with *their* eyes, and hear with *their* ears, and should understand with *their* heart, and should be converted,"

Mainly, these societies' hearts are repugnant as their souls are shallow to hear truths of Love. Not to mention, with their eyes closed to others, refusing to listen to facts upon their true nature of surrendering to our Lord who gave his life for Love and truth.

To this end, shall they follow the teachings of Christ to unfold spiritual truths that they may see and hear of spiritual truths within the wind of influences, thus leaning on the heart of true wealth?

Then, they shall obtain knowledge and understanding of their true nature of being.

Comment appropriately to "and I should heal them."

And to this end, *Christ* shall indeed heal them into the consciousness of God's Kingdom.

KJV Matthew 13: verse 16

But blessed *are* your eyes, for they see: and your ears, for they hear.

Comment appropriately to "But blessed *are* your eyes, for they see: and your ears, for they hear."

Thus, glorify the eye in spirit that sees all truths; blessed are the ears of the soul that hears all facts.

KJV Matthew 13: verse 17

For verily I say unto you, That many prophets and righteous *men* have desired to see *those things* which ye see, and have not seen *them*; and to hear *those things* which ye hear, and have not heard *them*.

Comment appropriately to "For verily I say unto you, That many prophets and righteous *men* have desired to see *those things* which ye see, and have not seen *them*;"

Indeed, you are choosing to accept truths on entering the kingdom of God, many followers of Christ, and leaders of the church.

Many followers of Christ and leaders of the houses of worship desire to seek truths leading to enlightenment.

Notwithstanding, they wish to see these things nonetheless will not because of their hidden motives from the actual teachings of Christ.

Note: Notice how righteous *men* "spelled with men" and not "man" makes us aware of a physical person—those unwilling to do the works sent by the Father through the Son of man.

Comment appropriately to "and to hear *those things* which ye hear, and have not heard *them*."

In addition, many will not hear truths from heaven as the enlightened soul as you have listened to it.

KJV Matthew 13: verse 18

Hear ye therefore the parable of the sower.

Comment appropriately to "Hear ye therefore the parable of the sower."

Again, become aware of truths for entering the kingdom of

heaven.

KJV Matthew 13: verse 19

When any one heareth the word of the kingdom, and understandeth *it* not, then cometh the wicked *one*, and catcheth away that which was sown in his heart. This is he which received seed by the way side.

Comment appropriately to "When any one heareth the word of the kingdom, and understandeth it not, then cometh the wicked *one*,"

When one is unaccepting of my (Jesus) teachings in the New Commandments to enter the kingdom, these souls will not understand the words of spirit and its content because of their alter-ego devilish minds.

Comment appropriately to "and catcheth away that which was sown in his heart. This is he which received seed by the way side."

Nonetheless, the lowly heart soul felt the sincerity in the heart which laid a seed of wealth yet, upon accepting the teachings because it sounded righteous.

KJV Matthew 13: verse 20

But he that received the seed into stony places, the same is he that heareth the word, and anon with joy receiveth it;

Comment appropriately to "But he that received the seed into stony places, the same is he that heareth the word, and anon with joy receiveth it;"

Therefore, when you hear kind words (seeds) of Love and guidance, which are spirit and not hurtful insults (stones) of disbelief of Christ our Lord. You accept its uprightness with inner joy and bliss from the sincerity of God's truths.

KJV Matthew 13: verse 21

Yet hath he not root in himself, but dureth for a while: for when tribulation or persecution ariseth because of the word, by and by he is offended.

Comment appropriately to "Yet hath he not root in himself, but dureth for a while: for when tribulation or persecution ariseth because of the word, by and by he is offended."

However, when you hear and understand (rooted) these truths in the teachings in the New Testament. The soul takes joy and happiness briefly because these revelations resonate within the core of your spirit.

At the same time, when a disturbance in the subconscious mind (human mind) questions the validity of what you can't understand in the teachings.

These insults will more than likely come from the spiritually dead (soul's unwillingness to accept Jesus' teachings as truth).

Contrarily, you may feel oppression in mind with doubts about the Commandments, which at times seem unthinkable or unrealistic to understand. But even more so, how could such a possibility exist when desiring to find the kingdom of

God.

Thus, inwardly, you become angry or even exasperated (offended).

KJV Matthew 13: verse 22

He also that received seed among the thorns is he that heareth the word; and the care of this world, and the deceitfulness of riches, choke the word, and he becometh unfruitful.

Comment appropriately to "He also that received seed among the thorns is he that heareth the word;"

However, he accepts righteous thinking (seed) amid unrighteous thoughts (thorns) and has indeed heard my voice in spirit.

Comment appropriately to "and the care of this world, and the deceitfulness of riches, choke the word, and he becometh unfruitful."

Therefore, give no thought to the physical appearance, which can mislead (deceitfulness) you down to false truths which suffocate spiritual knowledge. Thus, leaving you with untruths and unrighteousness (unfruitful).

KJV Matthew 13: verse 23

But he that received seed into the good ground is he that heareth the word, and understandeth *it*; which also beareth fruit, and bringeth forth, some an hundredfold, some sixty, some thirty.

Comment appropriately to "But he that received seed into the good ground is he that heareth the word, and understandeth *it*; which also beareth fruit, "

Finally, the spiritual soul hears and accepts the teachings upon the inner workings of the subconscious mind, which does the work (understands) from the Father.

To this end, it delivers and shares to others knowledge and understanding.

Comment appropriately to "and bringeth forth, some an hundredfold, some sixty, some thirty."

In addition, he enables a higher vibration of Loved one hundred times more, some sixty times more, and some thirty times more of their value of understanding.

KJV Matthew 13: verse 24

Another parable put he forth unto them, saying, The kingdom of heaven is likened unto a man which sowed good seed in his field:

Comment appropriately to "The kingdom of heaven is likened unto a man which sowed good seed in his field:"

The kingdom of heaven is as a man with the purity of thoughts (seed) within the subconscious mind (field) sharing abundant Love to all.

KJV Matthew 13: verse 25

But while men slept, his enemy came and sowed tares among

the wheat, and went his way.

Comment appropriately to "But while men slept, his enemy came and sowed tares among the wheat, and went his way."

Notwithstanding, while he was walking in darkness or lack of understanding (slept) or spiritually dead, his altered ego-mind (human mind believing he is the body) came in left doubts (tares) with the righteous thinking (wheat) as he continued his journey.

KJV Matthew 13: verse 26

But when the blade was sprung up, and brought forth fruit, then appeared the tares also.

Comment appropriately to "But when the blade was sprung up, and brought forth fruit, then appeared the tares also."

However, when the servants (angels) descended to the soul to bring out (sprung up) knowledge from the subconscious mind of the teachings of God.

Thus, doubts (tares) and worries also appeared in mind-blocking understanding.

KJV Matthew 13: verse 27

So the servants of the householder came and said unto him, Sir, didst not thou sow good seed in thy field? from whence then hath it tares?

Comment appropriately to "So the servants of the

householder came and said unto him, Sir, didst not thou sow good seed in thy field? from whence then hath it tares?"

Likewise, our Father's angels (servants) came to relay a message to God with Love, thus saying. Lord, did you not sow great abundant ideas and knowledge (good seed) in the subconscious mind of thy child?

Lord, how did the doubt (tares) come to this child's mind?

Special Note: Grace knows no abound, which indicates, our Father in heaven **did not** give us a fear-based energy vibration. In this non-destructible energy field of oneness, we are a resonant vibration of pure Love.

In a like manner, to hold on to fear-based energies are a violation of spiritual truths.

KJV Matthew 13: verse 28

He said unto them, An enemy hath done this. The servants said unto him, Wilt thou then that we go and gather them up?

Comment appropriately to "He said unto them, An enemy hath done this. The servants said unto him, Wilt thou then that we go and gather them up?"

Indeed, our Lord Jesus said unto the angels, the devil (metaphorically speaking) has inserted this low vibrational energy field (doubt in mind) in which I do not recognize.

Note: Considering this, our Lord and Savior are making us aware of the energy resonant vibration of pure Love when praying. Thus, with stillness in meditation, God's Love in cleansing alignment with his purpose for your life and not yours.

KJV Matthew 13: verse 29

But he said, Nay; lest while ye gather up the tares, ye root up also the wheat with them.

Comment appropriately to "But he said, Nay; lest while ye gather up the tares, ye root up also the wheat with them."

Thus says the Lord, no (Nay). Our Lord does not assemble righteous thinking (wheat) with doubts (tares).

KJV Matthew 13: verse 30

Let both grow together until the harvest: and in the time of harvest I will say to the reapers, Gather ye together first the tares, and bind them in bundles to burn them: but gather the wheat into my barn.

Comment appropriately to "Let both grow together until the harvest: and in the time of harvest I will say to the reapers, Gather ye together first the tares, and bind them in bundles to burn them: but gather the wheat into my barn."

The Lord said, allow the soul to continue its journey until the end of days (physical death of the body) when the time comes to appear before the gathering (harvest) of the righteousness of spiritual truths.

Accordingly, I'll advise the counsel and servants (reapers) to round up first all doubts and tie up (bind) into one area of the alter ego (human mind) to destroy all its lies (burn them) within subconsciousness.

In addition, tie up and gather all the moral truths (wheat) in the conscious mind of facts.

Special Note: Ascended guides are higher in spirits which serve as counsel in heaven which in most cases do not take incarnations on this earthly plane.

KJV Matthew 13: verse 31

Another parable put he forth unto them, saying, The kingdom of heaven is like to a grain of mustard seed, which a man took, and sowed in his field:

Comment appropriately to "The kingdom of heaven is like to a grain of mustard seed, which a man took, and sowed in his field:"

Indeed, the kingdom of heaven is like a little bit of wisdom (grain) of righteous thinking (mustard seed) which a spiritual being gathered and planted into his subconscious mind (field).

KJV Matthew 13: verse 32

Which indeed is the least of all seeds: but when it is grown, it is the greatest among herbs, and becometh a tree, so that the birds of the air come and lodge in the branches thereof.

Comment appropriately to "Which indeed is the least of all seeds: but when it is grown, it is the greatest among herbs,"

Nonetheless, it is the slightest bit of wisdom in the kingdom. However, when it advances within the domain, how mighty the great seed (herb) has become subconscious.

Comment appropriately to "and becometh a tree, so that the birds of the air come and lodge in the branches thereof."

Thus, it does indeed provide spiritual truths (tree) for the spiritual souls searching for facts (birds of the air) to gather and lean on (lodge) to expand consciously in thoughts leading to righteous thinking.

KJV Matthew 13: verse 33

Another parable spake he unto them; The kingdom of heaven is like unto leaven, which a woman took, and hid in three measures of meal, till the whole was leavened.

Comment appropriately to "The kingdom of heaven is like unto leaven, which a woman took, and hid in three measures of meal, till the whole was leavened."

Jesus is alerting the elect of disciples desiring to enter the kingdom of heaven. Subsequently, the domain is like an abundance of spiritual knowledge (bread) that the conscious mind of the Self (woman) had in her possession.

She (conscious mind) buried righteous thoughts in small amounts, which grew to medium quantities, which flourished until wholeness in knowledge (leaven).

KJV Matthew 13: verse 37

He answered and said unto them, He that soweth the good

seed is the Son of man;

Comment appropriately to "He that soweth the good seed is the Son of man;"

Indeed, he keeps righteous thoughts in mind that are certainly within the Son of man (body of Christ).

KJV Matthew 13: verse 38

The field is the world; the good seed are the children of the kingdom; but the tares are the children of the wicked *one*;

Comment appropriately to "The field is the world; the good seed are the children of the kingdom; but the tares are the children of the wicked *one*;"

First, the subconscious mind (field) is your inner world. Thus, in all abundance, the sower of the good seed is our Lord the Messiah planting righteous thoughts to the children of God, leading to Love in the subconscious mind.

Lastly, doubts (tares) lead to fear of awareness in the alter ego (human mind), prevailing to a wrongful type of thinking bonded with untruths and unrighteousness.

Hence, (the wicked one) (devil metaphor) portraying evil as the human mind's enemy of destructive thoughts, believing it is the human body and not a spiritual being—planted seed upon the world within.

KJV Matthew 13: verse 39

The enemy that sowed them is the devil; the harvest is the

end of the world; and the reapers are the angels.

Comment appropriately to "The enemy that sowed them is the devil; the harvest is the end of the world; and the reapers are the angels."

Certainly, the adversary who planted it was indeed the evil one; the alter ego (human mind) portrays both good and evil will meet judgment at the end of the day (physical death).

Notwithstanding, the servants (angels) will indeed gather the harvest (spiritual knowledge) for thy Lord.

KJV Matthew 13: verse 40

As therefore the tares are gathered and burned in the fire; so shall it be in the end of this world.

Comment appropriately to "As therefore the tares are gathered and burned in the fire; so shall it be in the end of this world."

Indeed, doubts (tares) are assembled and destroyed because of torment (hell's fire) the inner purity of thoughts. Thus, it will bring an end to untruths at the end of this soul's journey.

KJV Matthew 13: verse 41

The Son of man shall send forth his angels, and they shall gather out of his kingdom all things that offend, and them which do iniquity;

Comment appropriately to "The Son of man shall send forth his angels,"

For this reason, our Lord will send helpers (angles) into the field of consciousness.

Comment appropriately to "and they shall gather out of his kingdom all things that offend, and them which do iniquity"

For Love will assemble all righteousness in the kingdom (mind) all things which do not display light within the conscious thought. Furthermore, do away those unrighteous thoughts (iniquity) at once.

KJV Matthew 13: verse 42

And shall cast them into a furnace of fire: there shall be wailing and gnashing of teeth.

Comment appropriately to "And shall cast them into a furnace of fire: there shall be wailing and gnashing of teeth."

For Jesus said, I will cast out lies (furnace of fire) of this world, leaving it to all its untruths believing in earthly riches or material goods.

Notwithstanding, without realizing spiritual wealth is true wealth, there will be deep sorrow (wailing) in the soul and resentment (gnashing of teeth) of not following the teachings of Christ leading to the kingdom.

KJV Matthew 13: verse 43

Then shall the righteous shine forth as the sun in the kingdom of their Father. Who hath ears to hear, let him hear.

Comment appropriately to "Then shall the righteous shine forth as the sun in the kingdom of their Father."

Always shall all the anointed children of God let their understanding shine in the morning of Day (completion of enlightenment) before the Father's kingdom of heaven.

Comment appropriately to "Who hath ears to hear, let him hear."

Jesus alerts those willing to accept the truths behind the teachings given unto him from the Father on entering the kingdom. Nonetheless, those willing to accept these spiritual truths (ears to hear), let them hear.

KJV Matthew 13: verse 44

Again, the kingdom of heaven is like unto treasure hid in a field; the which when a man hath found, he hideth, and for joy thereof goeth and selleth all that he hath, and buyeth that field.

Comment appropriately to "Again, the kingdom of heaven is like unto treasure hid in a field; the which when a man hath found, he hideth,"

Likewise, the kingdom of heaven is comparable to having righteous thoughts (treasure) in the subconscious mind (field) and when you find what is rightfully yours.

You keep it seamlessly joyful within your heart for no one to take it away.

Comment appropriately to "and for joy thereof goeth and

selleth all that he hath, and buyeth that field."

Above all, you take this excitement of finding Love so profoundly for your Lord; you discard all your worldly attachments (sell inward desires of material needs in mind).

To obtain more (buy) conscious awareness in the freeing of the mind from bondage of this earth plain.

KJV Matthew 13: verse 45

Again, the kingdom of heaven is like unto a merchant man, seeking goodly pearls:

Comment appropriately to "Again, the kingdom of heaven is like unto a merchant man, seeking goodly pearls:"

Indeed, the kingdom of heaven is equivalent to son of God (a child anointed by Holy Spirit) seeking more Love by the ***Universal Law of Divine Flow***.

Note: To understand this principle, one must clearly understand the Law Giving and Receiving; thus, you get back precisely or more than you gave away spiritually with energy. However, in this case, energy flows where attention goes which is more love. (Divine Flow).

KJV Matthew 13: verse 46

Who, when he had found one pearl of great price, went and sold all that he had, and bought it.

Comment appropriately to "Who, when he had found one pearl of great price, went and sold all that he had, and bought it."

Once he found consciousness of the Self, the elect once gave away all worldliness and attachments to obtain enlightenment.

KJV Matthew 13: verse 47

Again, the kingdom of heaven is like unto a net, that was cast into the sea, and gathered of every kind:

Comment appropriately to "Again, the kingdom of heaven is like unto a net, that was cast into the sea, and gathered of every kind:"

For this purpose, the kingdom of heaven is that of a man seeking righteousness (net) outside of himself (cast into the sea). He sought truths in churches, houses of Prayer, temples, mosques, and synagogues.

KJV Matthew 13: verse 48

Which, when it was full, they drew to shore, and sat down, and gathered the good into vessels, but cast the bad away.

Comment appropriately to "Which, when it was full, they drew to shore, and sat down,"

As a result, he felt he had learned enough to enter God's kingdom (when it was full). As with many, when the time comes for the ending of days (sat down).

The lowly souls felt he had filled their storehouse (drawn to shore) however, it was with unrighteous teachings of the confusion of Godly men.

Comment appropriately to "and gathered the good into vessels, but cast the bad away."

Thus, what wee bit of righteousness he was usable was stored (the vessel is the subconscious mind); yet servants (God's angels) discarded the lies and untruths (bad) from all consciousness.

KJV Matthew 13: verse 49

So shall it be at the end of the world: the angels shall come forth, and sever the wicked from among the just,

Comment appropriately to "So shall it be at the end of the world: the angels shall come forth, and sever the wicked from among the just,"

Consequently, this is how it will be upon physical death of the body (end of the world).

Therefore, the servants will come in heaven and divide righteousness in thought from the unrighteousness from the spirit.

KJV Matthew 13: verse 50

And shall cast them into the furnace of fire: there shall be wailing and gnashing of teeth.

Comment appropriately to "And shall cast them into the furnace of fire: there shall be wailing and gnashing of teeth."

Nonetheless, they will rid all unrighteousness, untruths, and lies (furnace of fire) from the spirit.

Thus, there will be deep sorrow (wailing) in the soul and resentment (gnashing of teeth) of not following the teachings of Christ.

KJV Matthew 13: verse 51

Jesus saith unto them, Have ye understood all these things? They say unto him, Yea, Lord.

Comment appropriately to "Have ye understood all these things?"

Our Lord and Savior are bringing forth spiritual truths with the intent to hide before men who do not accept these teachings for entering the kingdom of heaven.

KJV Matthew 13: verse 52

Then said he unto them, Therefore every scribe *which is* instructed unto the kingdom of heaven is like unto a man *that is* an householder, which bringeth forth out of his treasure *things* new and old.

Comment appropriately to "Therefore every scribe *which is* instructed unto the kingdom of heaven is like unto a man *that is* an householder, which bringeth forth out of his treasure *things* new and old."

Indeed, every mind in consciousness (scribe) is directed in the kingdom of heaven to co-create life during its journey. Considering this, bring forth purpose out of the heart Love (treasures) of creation in consciousness (new) and subconsciously (old).

KJV Matthew 13: verse 57

And they were offended in him. But Jesus said unto them, A prophet is not without honour, save in his own country, and in his own house.

Comment appropriately to "And they were offended in him. But Jesus said unto them, A prophet is not without honour, save in his own country, and in his own house."

Accordingly, Jesus spoke, saying a prophet who desires to give truths but cannot be received (without honor) in his soul with those familiar with him. However, he must remain trustworthy within his soul as he continues unfolding conscious awareness (country).

Matthew Chapter 14

KJV Matthew 14: verse 16

But Jesus said unto them, They need not depart; give ye them to eat.

Comment appropriately to "They need not depart; give ye them to eat."

The followers of Jesus do not need to search elsewhere for righteous fruit.

KJV Matthew 14: verse 18

He said, Bring them hither to me.

Comment appropriately to "Bring them hither to me."

Bring forth all souls (fish) to me from the Father.

KJV Matthew 14: verse 27

But straightway Jesus spake unto them, saying, Be of good cheer; it is I; be not afraid.

Comment appropriately to "Be of good cheer; it is I; be not afraid."

Thus says the Lord always, be cheerful for, in me, you should not be afraid because of my enduring Love.

KJV Matthew 14: verse 29

And he said, Come. And when Peter was come down out of the ship, he walked on the water, to go to Jesus.

Comment appropriately to "Come."

In essence, come as you are, I thy Lord Jesus will make you whole.

KJV Matthew 14: verse 31

And immediately Jesus stretched forth *his* hand, and caught him, and said unto him, O thou of little faith, wherefore didst thou doubt?

Comment appropriately to "O thou of little faith, wherefore didst thou doubt?"

Therefore, you have no faith in the Lord, and how did this doubt arise in the subconscious mind?

Matthew Chapter 15

KJV Matthew 15: verse 3

But he answered and said unto them, Why do ye also transgress the commandment of God by your tradition?

Comment appropriately to "Why do ye also transgress the commandment of God by your tradition?"

To this end, why do you follow age-old traditions given to you by men that violate my New Commandments from the Father, which are righteous?

KJV Matthew 15: verse 4

For God commanded, saying, Honour thy father and mother: and, He that curseth father or mother, let him die the death.

Comment appropriately to "For God commanded, saying, Honour thy father and mother:"

Indeed, our Father in Heaven commands us to Honor Him and him only. So, likewise, honor your conscious mind (mother), which certainly is our one shared mind.

Comment appropriately to "and, He that curseth father or mother, let him die the death."

For the soul in darkness, he blasphemed (curseth) the Father who loves you or the mother, which is (Heaven). So shall indeed remain in darkness.

KJV Matthew 15: verse 5

But ye say, Whosoever shall say to *his* father or *his* mother, *It i*s a gift, by whatsoever thou mightest be profited by me;

Comment appropriately to "But ye say, Whosoever shall say to *his* father or *his* mother, *It is* a gift, by whatsoever thou mightest be profited by me;"

However, the Lord says anyone who accepts or announces Heavenly Father or Heaven is by Love we receive. Wherefore, thy Lord God shall bring forth wealth from consciousness in the name of our Lord Jesus Christ.

Note: Indeed, when asking in the "name of Jesus." we bring forth the righteous meaning for what we ask for in Love on our soul's journey.

Thus, in Jesus' name is believing in Christ as Lord one in the Father, and therefore you're asking is in sincerity less hidden motives and shall be honored with Love.

KJV Matthew 15: verse 6

And honour not his father or his mother, *he shall be free*. Thus have ye made the commandment of God of none effect by your tradition.

Comment appropriately to "And honour not his father or his mother, *he shall be free."*

Therefore, you will not be set free in mind if you do not honor your Heavenly Father or Heaven the conscious mind (mother) accepting these as truths.

Comment appropriately to "Thus have ye made the commandment of God of none effect by your tradition."

As a result, you have followed inadequate traditions, which are meaningless as you do them blindly to God's new commandments.

Note: Traditions begin as ideas manifested to earthly riches by evildoers who portray sympathetic logic. When we don't question traditions and even holidays, we miss or evade God's purpose in our life.

We end up following others blindly, not understanding why we do as others do without questioning its value.

KJV Matthew 15: verse 7

Ye hypocrites, well did Esaias prophesy of you, saying,

Comment appropriately to "*Ye* hypocrites, well did Esaias prophesy of you, saying,"

You're a deceiver (hypocrite), Isaiah (Esaias) announced these events were saying.

KJV Matthew 15: verse 8

This people draweth nigh unto me with their mouth, and honoureth me with *their* lips; but their heart is far from me.

Comment appropriately to "This people draweth nigh unto me with their mouth, and honoureth me with *their* lips; but their heart is far from me."

Men of the cloth come unto me with their preaching and prayers by the babbling mouth. However, inwardly, they are far from the kingdom of Heaven.

KJV Matthew 15: verse 9

But in vain they do worship me, teaching *for* doctrines the commandments of men.

Comment appropriately to "But in vain they do worship me, teaching *for* doctrines the commandments of men."

Consequently, they are far from my teachings of righteousness (vain worship). However, they were also leaning to their understanding, making rules fit their ideas of what is suitable for all.

KJV Matthew 15: verse 10

And he called the multitude, and said unto them, Hear, and understand:

Comment appropriately to "Hear, and understand:"

Thus, the Lord says, take heed not to follow others blindly and understand you were made consciously for spirit revelations.

KJV Matthew 15: verse 11

Not that which goeth into the mouth defileth a man; but that which cometh out of the mouth, this defileth a man.

Comment appropriately to "Not that which goeth into the mouth defileth a man; but that which cometh out of the mouth, this defileth a man."

Furthermore, regardless of what enters the mouth will not dishonor the man.

However, that unworthy speech or language which comes from the heart is what gives him dishonorable intentions.

KJV Matthew 15: verse 13

But he answered and said, Every plant, which my heavenly Father hath not planted, shall be rooted up.

Comment appropriately to "Every plant, which my heavenly Father hath not planted, shall be rooted up."

Therefore, every unrighteous doctrine (plant) which corrupts an action shall be removed from the mind by the Father on the last day.

KJV Matthew 15: verse 14

Let them alone: they be blind leaders of the blind. And if the blind lead the blind, both shall fall into the ditch.

Comment appropriately to "Let them alone: they be blind leaders of the blind. And if the blind lead the blind, both shall fall into the ditch."

In other words, let them be in their mind's thoughts; because they do not accept the teachings of God, they'll remain in darkness from the kingdom of Heaven.

In addition, if they are blind and leading others who do not question their faith, then both will fall into the darkness searching the kingdom of God.

KJV Matthew 15: verse 16

And Jesus said, Are ye also yet without understanding?

Comment appropriately to "Are ye also yet without understanding?"

Our Lord is saying to those who are unaccepting of his teaching, are you able to discern my speech because they are spiritual truths.

KJV Matthew 15: verse 17

Do not ye yet understand, that whatsoever entereth in at the mouth goeth into the belly, and is cast out into the draught?

Comment appropriately to "Do not ye yet understand, that whatsoever entereth in at the mouth goeth into the belly, and is cast out into the draught?"

Thus says Jesus, do you not understand the inner workings of the heart? So, therefore, whatever enters the mouth goes into the stomach and finds its way on the bottom outwardly.

KJV Matthew 15: verse 18

But those things which proceed out of the mouth come forth from the heart; and they defile the man.

Comment appropriately to "But those things which proceed out of the mouth come forth from the heart; and they defile the man."

However, the rhetoric that comes out of the mouth comes from the heart through the subconscious mind in thought. For this reason, this is what truly dishonors a man.

KJV Matthew 15: verse 19

For out of the heart proceed evil thoughts, murders, adulteries, fornications, thefts, false witness, blasphemies:

Comment appropriately to "For out of the heart proceed evil thoughts, murders, adulteries, fornications, thefts, false witness, blasphemies:"

Accordingly, unrighteous thinking comes from the heart through the alter ego (human mind)—such misdeeds of misuse, immorality, wrongful intimacy, thievery, con artist, and injustice.

KJV Matthew 15: verse 20

These are *the things* which defile a man: but to eat with unwashen hands defileth not a man.

Comment appropriately to "These are *the things* which defile a man: but to eat with unwashen hands defileth not a man."

As a result, these are the things such unrighteous thoughts dishonor a man. Not the simplifying effect of not washing one's hands.

KJV Matthew 15: verse 24

But he answered and said, I am not sent but unto the lost sheep of the house of Israel.

Comment appropriately to "I am not sent but unto the lost sheep of the house of Israel."

For this purpose, my presence is for the lost children (sheep) near the souls (house) earthly kingdom (house of Israel).

KJV Matthew 15: verse 26

But he answered and said, It is not meet to take the children's bread, and to cast *it* to dogs.

Comment appropriately to "It is not meet to take the children's bread, and to cast *it* to dogs."

Hence, it isn't conventional to give knowledge (spiritual food - bread) of truth to those unaccepting (dogs) the teachings of Christ.

KJV Matthew 15: verse 28

Then Jesus answered and said unto her, O woman, great is thy faith: be it unto thee even as thou wilt. And her daughter was made whole from that very hour.

Comment appropriately to "O woman, great *is* thy faith: be it unto thee even as thou wilt."

In this parable, we reflect on verse twenty-six of this chapter. Nonetheless, a daughter asks for healing as the Messiah renounces her faith in lack of repentance but believing in Christ as the Son of God.

Jesus allows mercy in her repentance in the heart, thus by faith. Therefore, her request in prayer was granted.

KJV Matthew 15: verse 32

Then Jesus called his disciples *unto him*, and said, I have compassion on the multitude, because they continue with me now three days, and have nothing to eat: and I will not send them away fasting, lest they faint in the way.

Comment appropriately to "I have compassion on the multitude, because they continue with me now three days, and have nothing to eat: and I will not send them away fasting, lest they faint in the way."

While sharing the gospels and the teachings, Jesus said, with Love for my flock on this journey, we are manifesting a soul's cycles of desire on day three (evening, Night, morning, and Day)

Note: There are four cycles in a soul's journey to enlightenment. Jesus is referring to the soul's journey and not three days with him in the physical.

They had not eaten spiritual food (knowledge); thus, to send them away fasting would mean from worldly attachments by transcendental meditation.

In doing so, they would perish unfamiliar spiritual teachings given recently by the Messiah on entering the kingdom.

KJV Matthew 15: verse 34

And Jesus saith unto them, How many loaves have ye? And they said, Seven, and a few little fishes.

Comment appropriately to "How many loaves have ye?"

In this parable, the Messiah is raising awareness to his disciples on the true teacher of men.

Thus, the Lord Jesus is one teacher; he is the leaven or bread keeper of knowledge and understanding.

Matthew Chapter 16

KJV Matthew 16: verse 2

He answered and said unto them, When it is evening, ye say, *It will be* fair weather: for the sky is red.

Comment appropriately to "When it is evening, ye say, *It will be* fair weather: for the sky is red."

Thus, our Lord Jesus' teaching continues by giving insight into a soul's journey to enlightenment. Each season in the cycle merges into the next season, for instance.

The evening-Night-morning, and then Day (completion) and in this case of this parable. Jesus is awakening inner light upon a soul's path in his name.

For which path this moment (evening) has passed, for it is the sign of lowliness of evening warmth (weather) where the spirit is unconcerned.

(*These are part of the actual teachings of Jesus Christ - f*or they are spiritual).

KJV Matthew 16: verse 3

And in the morning, *It will be* foul weather to day: for the sky is red and lowring. O *ye* hypocrites, ye can discern the face of the sky; but can ye not *discern* the signs of the times?

Comment appropriately to "And in the morning, *It will be* foul weather to day: for the sky is red and lowring. O *ye* hypocrites,"

Again, a soul's journey by day (to day) "small d" not "Day" desires complete; of the morning to dawn (evening) likened to warmth. Thus, the foul weather on a soul's journey could indicate seasons on despair, lost, unable to confer clear direction.

In other words, evening "day" at dusk leading into night or darkness. Whence, no soul can work.

However, this alignment of spiritual truths of the Day when the sky is red with warmth and descending (lowering) to evening. Oh, ye deceivers who long for the kingdom.

Comment appropriately to "ye can discern the face of the sky; but can ye not *discern* the signs of the times?"

Moreover, you cannot know spiritual truth by looking at the sky to understand a soul's journey by waiting on a sign from a fortune teller.

KJV Matthew 16: verse 4

A wicked and adulterous generation seeketh after a sign; and there shall no sign be given unto it, but the sign of the prophet

Jonas. And he left them, and departed.

Comment appropriately to "A wicked and adulterous generation seeketh after a sign; and there shall no sign be given unto it, but the sign of the prophet Jonas."

An unrighteous and immoral generation is always seeking proof to verify their evil way of thinking. For this, you will not see or witness any signs as the prophet Jonas did as a testimony.

KJV Matthew 16: verse 6

Then Jesus said unto them, Take heed and beware of the leaven of the Pharisees and of the Sadducees.

Comment appropriately to "Take heed and beware of the leaven of the Pharisees and of the Sadducees."

Similarly, take notice and avoid the authority of lessons (leaven) from the evangelist and ministers.

KJV Matthew 16: verse 8

Which when Jesus perceived, he said unto them, O ye of little faith, why reason ye among yourselves, because ye have brought no bread?

Comment appropriately to "O ye of little faith, why reason ye among yourselves, because ye have brought no bread?"

More importantly, why do you have so little belief in thy Lord? Why debate amongst yourselves because you wonder to whom or where this spiritual knowledge (bread) will come too?

KJV Matthew 16: verse 9

Do ye not yet understand, neither remember the five loaves of the five thousand, and how many baskets ye took up?

Comment appropriately to "Do ye not yet understand, neither remember the five loaves of the five thousand, and how many baskets ye took up?"

Thus, do you not perceive spiritual knowledge (understanding) and believe not in the Lord thy God Jesus?

Even as he provided leaven of spiritual food for the spiritual body of five thousand and filled their being as you witnessed.

KJV Matthew 16: verse 10

Neither the seven loaves of the four thousand, and how many baskets ye took up?

Comment appropriately to "Neither the seven loaves of the four thousand, and how many baskets ye took up?"

By witnesses, still, perceive with little faith the leaven for four thousand souls filled with spiritual food as you gathered plenty of knowledge (bread baskets) additionally for yourselves.

KJV Matthew 16: verse 11

How is it that ye do not understand that I spake *it* not to you concerning bread, that ye should beware of the leaven of the

Pharisees and of the Sadducees?

Comment appropriately to "How is it that ye do not understand that I spake *it* not to you concerning bread, that ye should beware of the leaven of the Pharisees and of the Sadducees?"

Again, tell the Lord, how can you not understand a spiritual thing I speak when it contains knowledge of the spiritual realm?

In the same way, be mindful not to gain insight from a holy man (Pharisees and Sadducees) on their messages of true worship.

KJV Matthew 16: verse 13

When Jesus came into the coasts of Caesarea Philippi, he asked his disciples, saying, Whom do men say that I the Son of man am?

Comment appropriately to "Whom do men say that I the Son of man am?"

Consequently, of the followers, what do they say concerning the Son of man on who am I?

KJV Matthew 16: verse 15

He saith unto them, But whom say ye that I am?

Comment appropriately to "But whom say ye that I am?"

Likewise, in the same manner, who do you say I am?

KJV Matthew 16: verse 17

And Jesus answered and said unto him, Blessed art thou, Simon Barjona: for flesh and blood hath not revealed *it* unto thee, but my Father which is in heaven.

Comment appropriately to "Blessed art thou, Simon Barjona: for flesh and blood hath not revealed *it* unto thee, but my Father which is in heaven"

Indeed, Simon Barjona, for the spiritual body (flesh) of Christ and resurrection (blood) which reveals all spiritual truths from the Son given by the Father in Heaven.

KJV Matthew 16: verse 18

And I say also unto thee, That thou art Peter, and upon this rock I will build my church; and the gates of hell shall not prevail against it.

Comment appropriately to "And I say also unto thee, That thou art Peter, and upon this rock I will build my church; and the gates of hell shall not prevail against it.

For this purpose, I give Peter Love and Truth (Rock) of glory to stand against the test of time. These truths form the teachings given unto the Son of man (the Messiah) for which my testament is spirit.

Holds (gate) all truth not allowing the subconscious (human mind) - hence, hell; shall not succeed against all righteousness.

KJV Matthew 16: verse 19

And I will give unto thee the keys of the kingdom of heaven: and whatsoever thou shalt bind on earth shall be bound in heaven: and whatsoever thou shalt loose on earth shall be loosed in heaven.

Comment appropriately to "And I will give unto thee the keys of the kingdom of heaven: and whatsoever thou shalt bind on earth shall be bound in heaven:"

Truthfully, I (thy Lord) will light the pathway to the kingdom of Heaven before you. Thus, everything you do not liberate in the heart and mind will remain unopened in consciousness.

Comment appropriately to "and whatsoever thou shalt loose on earth shall be loosed in heaven."

Likewise, what you liberate in the subconscious mind here upon planet earth, will also be released in conscious mind (Heaven).

KJV Matthew 16: verse 23

But he turned, and said unto Peter, Get thee behind me, Satan: thou art an offence unto me: for thou savourest not the things that be of God, but those that be of men.

Comment appropriately to "Get thee behind me, Satan: thou art an offence unto me: for thou savourest not the things that be of God, but those that be of men."

In other words, "Farewell Satan," because you are a hindrance for the righteousness purpose given unto me the Messiah by the Father on High. Your thoughts are not aligned with the spirit because it is portrayed as evil thinking in mind.

Note: Satan is used to characterize man's mind throughout the bible. However, it is metaphorically speaking, for there is only God and man.

KJV Matthew 16: verse 24

Then said Jesus unto his disciples, If any *man* will come after me, let him deny himself, and take up his cross, and follow me.

Comment appropriately to "If any *man* will come after me, let him deny himself, and take up his cross, and follow me."

Therefore, if anyone accepts my teachings given by spirit, allow yourself to surrender and concede (deny yourself) your life unto Christ for righteousness. Repent, and face yourself in the renewing of the mind away from unrighteous thinking.

Thus, follow me by accepting all truths that are in spirit.

KJV Matthew 16: verse 25

For whosoever will save his life shall lose it: and whosoever will lose his life for my sake shall find it.

Comment appropriately to "For whosoever will save his life shall lose it: and whosoever will lose his life for my sake shall find it."

Insincerity, if anyone tries to save themselves in the physical for any reason, they shall lose it. However, those willing to give a life for Jesus' sake shall indeed remain worthy of their life finding the kingdom.

KJV Matthew 16: verse 26

For what is a man profited, if he shall gain the whole world, and lose his own soul? or what shall a man give in exchange for his soul?

Comment appropriately to "For what is a man profited, if he shall gain the whole world, and lose his own soul?"

Indeed, for what good reason should a man gain earthly riches turning a blind eye to spiritual truths neglecting his soul, which is eternal.

Comment appropriately to "or what shall a man give in exchange for his soul?"

To this end, what is much worthier than your soul, for it is eternal. While nothing here as far as the eyes can see is admirable indeed!

KJV Matthew 16: verse 27

For the Son of man shall come in the glory of his Father with his angels; and then he shall reward every man according to his works.

Comment appropriately to "For the Son of man shall come in the glory of his Father with his angels;"

Enamored with triumph and elations in our Father, Christ

will be with the angels in celebration of victory.

Comment appropriately to "and then he shall reward every man according to his works."

Therefore, a spirit of rejoicing for every soul according to the works done in the subconscious mind.

KJV Matthew 16: verse 28

Verily I say unto you, There be some standing here, which shall not taste of death, till they see the Son of man coming in his kingdom.

Comment appropriately to "Verily I say unto you,"

Listen to this truth concerning entering the Kingdom of God.

Comment appropriately to "There be some standing here, which shall not taste of death, till they see the Son of man coming in his kingdom."

Truly I tell you that there will be believers of Christ that will not taste death (consciously aware of spirit) until they see their Lord coming into his kingdom.

Matthew Chapter 17

KJV Matthew 17: verse 7

And Jesus came and touched them, and said, Arise, and be not afraid.

Comment appropriately to "Arise, and be not afraid."

Awaken thy mind, be not afraid, for I am with you.

KJV Matthew 17: verse 9

And as they came down from the mountain, Jesus charged them, saying, Tell the vision to no man, until the Son of man be risen again from the dead.

Comment appropriately to "Tell the vision to no man, until the Son of man be risen again from the dead."

For this purpose, wrongdoers and doubters will question your validity of this vision on high. Thus, they will surely disappoint you inwardly by telling lies. As a result, say to no one until your Lord has risen from the dead.

KJV Matthew 17: verse 11

And Jesus answered and said unto them, Elias truly shall first come, and restore all things.

Comment appropriately to "Elias truly shall first come, and restore all things."

Consequently, it is written in the old times (Old Testament) concerning the one to end all suffering. Thus, Elias (John the Baptist) came in a manner to clear a way for the Messiah to those seeking repentance.

KJV Matthew 17: verse 12

But I say unto you, That Elias is come already, and they knew him not, but have done unto him whatsoever they listed. Likewise shall also the Son of man suffer of them.

Comment appropriately to "But I say unto you, That Elias is come already, and they knew him not, but have done unto him whatsoever they listed. Likewise shall also the Son of man suffer of them."

Indeed, I tell you Elias has come already in a different form of a body known as "John the Baptist." Yet, they didn't recognize the spirit of his inner soul because they did what evil men wanted and tormented his heart as they pleased.

In the same manner, the Son of man shall suffer likewise to fulfill scripture and rise again on the third day.

KJV Matthew 17: verse 17

Then Jesus answered and said, O faithless and perverse generation, how long shall I be with you? how long shall I suffer you? bring him hither to me.

Comment appropriately to "O faithless and perverse generation, how long shall I be with you? how long shall I suffer you? bring him hither to me."

On the contrary, how much longer will this society take in not accepting the Messiah is at hand? Oh, you do not believe what is standing right in front of you; how much longer must I remain patient with you?

Immediately, you must open your heart to receive truths for healing others in spirit. Bring forth those who are willing before me.

KJV Matthew 17: verse 20

And Jesus said unto them, Because of your unbelief: for verily I say unto you, If ye have faith as a grain of mustard seed, ye shall say unto this mountain, Remove hence to yonder place; and it shall remove; and nothing shall be impossible unto you.

Comment appropriately to "Because of your unbelief: for verily I say unto you, If ye have faith as a grain of mustard seed, ye shall say unto this mountain, Remove hence to yonder place;"

Nonetheless, because you have doubt lodged in the subconscious mind, you cannot reason with hidden motives discerning the resurrection power you hold within your spirit.

Therefore, I say concerning the kingdom of heaven if you hold faith as much as a mustard seed (unwavering thought). Then, indeed, you could say to the mountain (low vibrational thought), "move, for my Lord God's resurrection power is within me," Amen.

Comment appropriately to "and it shall remove; and nothing shall be impossible unto you."

Indeed, with faith and gratitude, it shall be moved. With God, all things are possible.

Note: Remember, the critical principle with faith is patience.

KJV Matthew 17: verse 21

Howbeit this kind goeth not out but by prayer and fasting.

Comment appropriately to "Howbeit this kind goeth not out but by prayer and fasting."

Be it as it may, non-believing cannot have the power of prayer belief or meditation inwardly work required by the Father.

KJV Matthew 17: verse 22

And while they abode in Galilee, Jesus said unto them, The Son of man shall be betrayed into the hands of men:

Comment appropriately to "The Son of man shall be

betrayed into the hands of men:"

In this parable, our Lord and Savior state, for a ransom of my sheep. He has forsaken me away from the hearts of men.

KJV Matthew 17: verse 23

And they shall kill him, and the third day he shall be raised again. And they were exceeding sorry.

Comment appropriately to "And they shall kill him, and the third day he shall be raised again."

They will crucify the Son of man, although dead in the physical and buried in all likeliness; nevertheless, he shall come to all glory and rise again on the third day.

KJV Matthew 17: verse 25

He saith, Yes. And when he was come into the house, Jesus prevented him, saying, What thinkest thou, Simon? of whom do the kings of the earth take custom or tribute? of their own children, or of strangers?

Comment appropriately to "What thinkest thou, Simon? of whom do the kings of the earth take custom or tribute? of their own children, or of strangers?"

Meanwhile, Jesus confronts Simon Peter while he is in the thought of wrongful doing of the tax collectors. Thus, the Lord of full consciousness is aware of all things to include reflections in the heart and mind.

The Lord asks Simon what emotions are in the subconscious

mind concerning rulers and evildoers who take what is rightfully yours?

Notwithstanding, do they take wages from their kind or to those provoked by fear?

KJV Matthew 17: verse 26

Peter saith unto him, Of strangers. Jesus saith unto him, Then are the children free.

Comment appropriately to "Then are the children free."

Accordingly, likewise, you are free as a child of the highest.

KJV Matthew 17: verse 27

Notwithstanding, lest we should offend them, go thou to the sea, and cast an hook, and take up the fish that first cometh up; and when thou hast opened his mouth, thou shalt find a piece of money: that take, and give unto them for me and thee.

Comment appropriately to "Notwithstanding, lest we should offend them, go thou to the sea, and cast an hook, and take up the fish that first cometh up;"

Nevertheless, with Love as our intent, we will not offend our adversaries. Therefore, as you believe in your heart and mind, go within your subconscious (sea) thoughts, and ask for what you desire (hook).

Thus, take the salvation (fish Jesus offers) of Love which comes first to the sense of your wish fulfilled.

Note: Indeed, this is the truth of how to pray.

Comment appropriately to "and when thou hast opened his mouth, thou shalt find a piece of money: that take, and give unto them for me and thee."

While in the prayer of asking the Father, accept the first word given: the spirit's wealth from heaven. Furthermore, bring your awareness in thoughts to me like thee.

Matthew Chapter 18

KJV Matthew 18: verse 3

And said, Verily I say unto you, Except ye be converted, and become as little children, ye shall not enter into the kingdom of heaven.

Comment appropriately to "Verily I say unto you,"

Most importantly, listen to what is necessary for entering the kingdom of heaven.

Comment appropriately to "Except ye be converted, and become as little children, ye shall not enter into the kingdom of heaven."

Until you transform the mind from the bondage of unrighteous thinking, remembering what it felt like as a child. Free from worry, doubt, emotional pain, you will not complete the renewing of the mind - which is spirit.

KJV Matthew 18: verse 4

Whosoever therefore shall humble himself as this little child, the same is greatest in the kingdom of heaven.

Comment appropriately to "Whosoever therefore shall humble himself as this little child, the same is greatest in the kingdom of heaven."

Wherefore, my convert, which serves everyone with Love in the humbling themselves, shall be most significant amongst all. So, likewise, as a child in the renewing of righteous thinking freed from bondage shall indeed enter the kingdom of heaven.

KJV Matthew 18: verse 5

And whoso shall receive one such little child in my name receiveth me.

Comment appropriately to "And whoso shall receive one such little child in my name receiveth me."

Therefore, whoever does my Father's work and receives the renewing of the mind (little child). So shall indeed receive me in the likeness of the Father.

KJV Matthew 18: verse 6

But whoso shall offend one of these little ones which believe in me, it were better for him that a millstone were hanged about his neck, and *that* he were drowned in the depth of the sea.

Comment appropriately to "But whoso shall offend one of these little ones which believe in me, it were better for him that a millstone were hanged about his neck,"

Consequently, whoever provokes (shall offend) a believer who confides in our Lord thus, in seeking the renewing (childlike mind full of laughter) of the mind. Indeed, you are better off avoiding self-affliction under **Universal Law of Challenge** (millstone around the neck).

Note: In this parable, our Lord brings awareness of how Universal Law affects those who use words profound abuse by affliction towards another. In other words, that painful affliction towards a child, and in this case, believer of Christ.

Will indeed manifest *double* because they (children of God) are willing to forgive the offender, which transcends those afflictions (energy) back to the sender.

Note: In other words, the inequity of persecution returns harshly in mind to lead the opposer back to Love by way of our Lord's **Universal Law of Unconditional Love**.

Comment appropriately to "and *that* he were drowned in the depth of the sea."

In essence, those inequities of the verbiage manifest (drown) in the adversary's subconscious mind (sea) to teach harmonies lessons of Love.

KJV Matthew 18: verse 7

Woe unto the world because of offences! for it must needs be that offences come; but woe to that man by whom the offence cometh!

Comment appropriately to "Woe unto the world because of offences! for it must needs be that offences come; but woe to that man by whom the offence cometh!"

Accordingly, misfortune (Woe) to the mind of the adversary, for unto him these same offenses return to him to teach a better way of Love. So, likewise, burdens in the subconscious mind of the gentle soul receiving these insults.

KJV Matthew 18: verse 8

Wherefore if thy hand or thy foot offend thee, cut them off, and cast *them* from thee: it is better for thee to enter into life halt or maimed, rather than having two hands or two feet to be cast into everlasting fire.

Comment appropriately to "Wherefore if thy hand or thy foot offend thee, cut them off, and cast *them* from thee:"

Therefore, while you are on your journey (foot), feel your heart (hand) broken from being hurt by another. So, remove (cast out) the damage by forgiving them instantly from thoughts entering the subconscious mind of memory.

Comment appropriately to "it is better for thee to enter into life halt or maimed, rather than having two hands or two feet to be cast into everlasting fire."

It is exceedingly wonderful to discover your true nature rather than keeping a bruised (maimed) heart. Otherwise, you see in your physical (two hands and feet) believing you are the body.

Consequently, it will eventually lead you not to seek truths within oneself, contrarily remaining in the alter ego (human mind).

KJV Matthew 18: verse 9

And if thine eye offend thee, pluck it out, and cast *it* from thee: it is better for thee to enter into life with one eye, rather than having two eyes to be cast into hell fire.

Comment appropriately to "And if thine eye offend thee, pluck it out, and cast *it* from thee:"

Permanently, if what you see is unrighteous, remove those thoughts (pluck it out) from your subconscious thinking because it is better to see with your third eye (mind's eye), which considers all truths.

Thus, having your physical body which sees all unrighteousness in the alter ego (human mind).

Comment appropriately to "it is better for thee to enter into life with one eye, rather than having two eyes to be cast into hell fire."

Therefore, it is far more significant to enter God's Kingdom with your mind's eye (third eye chakra) than to see what is unrighteous (two eyes) casting you into tormented thoughts in the human mind (hell's fire).

KJV Matthew 18: verse 10

Take heed that ye despise not one of these little ones; for I say unto you, That in heaven their angels do always behold the face of my Father which is in heaven.

Comment appropriately to "Take heed that ye despise not one of these little ones;"

Above all, do not give deep disgust towards a true believer (little ones) in the teachings of Christ.

Comment appropriately to "for I say unto you, That in heaven their angels do always behold the face of my Father which is in heaven."

For this is true concerning the kingdom of heaven thus, in consciousness their servants (angels) of my Father will indeed protect (behold the face) those seeking righteousness in teachings as Chosen ones.

KJV Matthew 18: verse 11

For the Son of man is come to save that which was lost.

Comment appropriately to "For the Son of man is come to save that which was lost."

Indeed, the Son of man cometh to save the subconsciousness of those willing to repent.

KJV Matthew 18: verse 12

How think ye? if a man have an hundred sheep, and one of them be gone astray, doth he not leave the ninety and nine, and goeth into the mountains, and seeketh that which is gone astray?

Comment appropriately to "How think ye? "

In dismay, can you not believe how much Love your Heavenly Father hold for his child? Are you unbelieving?

Comment appropriately to "if a man have an hundred sheep, and one of them be gone astray, doth he not leave the ninety and nine, and goeth into the mountains, and seeketh that which is gone astray?"

Indeed, the Shepard (Lord Jesus) has many followers, and if just one (one who seeks righteousness in the teachings) should hinder and fall away from his flock.

Honestly, the Good Shepherd (Jesus) will make way (leave the ninety-nine) to recover truth in the one in all consciousness (mountains) and in the subconscious mind where unrighteous thinking (gone astray) occurs.

KJV Matthew 18: verse 13

And if so be that he find it, verily I say unto you, he rejoiceth more of that *sheep*, than of the ninety and nine which went not astray.

Comment appropriately to "And if so be that he find it, verily I say unto you,"

Undoubtedly, once he regains righteous thinking in the one, truly I tell you this on seeking the kingdom of heaven.

Comment appropriately to "he rejoiceth more of that *sheep*, than of the ninety and nine which went not astray."

Gloriously I tell you that the Son of man exults the Father in Heaven of the one because he did not lose any of the others while lifting the one.

KJV Matthew 18: verse 14

Even so it is not the will of your Father which is in heaven, that one of these little ones should perish.

Comment appropriately to "Even so it is not the will of your Father which is in heaven, that one of these little ones should perish."

This is not our Father in heaven's will (Love and truth) that any believer in Christ should not succumb (perish) to the alter ego evil mind.

KJV Matthew 18: verse 15

Moreover if thy brother shall trespass against thee, go and tell him his fault between thee and him alone: if he shall hear thee, thou hast gained thy brother.

Comment appropriately to "Moreover if thy brother shall trespass against thee, go and tell him his fault between thee and him alone:"

Consequently, if your brother offends you with his thoughts or words, remember, before words, come within ideas - Hence, the Lord's Prayer, forgive those who trespass against us.

Specifically, forgive him immediately and make him aware of how those insults offended you in the heart while you are with him in private.

Comment appropriately to "if he shall hear thee, thou hast gained thy brother."

With this purpose in mind, once he has accepted his wrongdoing in thought towards you. Then, you have indeed regained your brother's Love.

KJV Matthew 18: verse 16

But if he will not hear *thee, then* take with thee one or two more, that in the mouth of two or three witnesses every word may be established.

Comment appropriately to "But if he will not hear *thee, then* take with thee one or two more, that in the mouth of two or three witnesses every word may be established."

Granted that, in haste to your opponent's inner anger does not release joy towards you. "Be still," and call upon your Heavenly Father, Son (Truth, 2), and Holy Spirit (Love, 3) (two or three) that the word of Love is deeply rooted (established).

Note: In short, in transcendental meditation (in the mouth of two or three), we must set our intentions to "God's will" and not our own. Of course, prayer and asking the spirit to intervene in this situation may bring about peace and a harmonious ending.

KJV Matthew 18: verse 17

And if he shall neglect to hear them, tell *it* unto the church: but if he neglect to hear the church, let him be unto thee as an heathen man and a publican.

Comment appropriately to "And if he shall neglect to hear them, tell *it* unto the church:"

Therefore, if your appointment with your opposer doesn't change (neglect to hear) thus, allow prayer to your Lord and the kingdom (church) to allow closure on the event or situation.

Comment appropriately to "but if he neglect to hear the church, let him be unto thee as an heathen man and a publican."

Suppose your opposer chooses to hold their Love away from you spiritually? Then, leave them to be (state of being), for they are spiritually dead (heathen man) and aren't worthy of your time pursuing the kingdom of heaven.

Note: The Lord's prayer serves as everlasting Love in the Father. Hence, peace is through conscious awareness that all things are of God.

In other words, let your peace rest with God in trinity, Father, Son, and Holy Ghost.

KJV Matthew 18: verse 18

Verily I say unto you, Whatsoever ye shall bind on earth shall be bound in heaven: and whatsoever ye shall loose on earth shall be loosed in heaven.

Comment appropriately to "Verily I say unto you,"

Follow my truths for entering the kingdom of heaven.

Comment appropriately to "Whatsoever ye shall bind on

earth shall be bound in heaven: and whatsoever ye shall loose on earth shall be loosed in heaven."

Therefore, the neglect of spiritual work during this incarnation (bind on earth) shall indeed return with you in your consciousness upon physical death.

In addition, the spiritual work you do accomplish (loose on earth) will indeed be glorified within your consciousness always!

KJV Matthew 18: verse 19

Again I say unto you, That if two of you shall agree on earth as touching any thing that they shall ask, it shall be done for them of my Father which is in heaven.

Comment appropriately to "Again I say unto you,"

For it is written in my teaching for entering the kingdom of heaven.

Comment appropriately to "That if two of you shall agree on earth as touching any thing that they shall ask, it shall be done for them of my Father which is in heaven."

Indeed, when thoughts and emotions subconsciously (on earth) are aligned (agreed in mind) in Christ, ask from the heart (touching). Through righteous asking without hidden motives through the spirit to the Father, which is in heaven.

Our Lord shall do it according to thy faith (belief).

KJV Matthew 18: verse 20

For where two or three are gathered together in my name, there am I in the midst of them.

Comment appropriately to "For where two or three are gathered together in my name, there am I in the midst of them."

Indeed, where thoughts and emotions (two), or seeing (visualizing) (three) are together in my name, there I am also.

KJV Matthew 18: verse 22

Jesus saith unto him, I say not unto thee, Until seven times: but, Until seventy times seven.

Comment appropriately to "I say not unto thee,"

In this meaning, understand my teachings.

Comment appropriately to "Until seven times: but, Until seventy times seven."

Indeed, align the spiritual body of the seven chakras **(seven times)** from the root chakra to the anointed crown chakra.

Thus, the **Root Chakra** (Muladhara), **Sacral Chakra** (Swadhisthana), **Solar Plexus Chakra** (Manipura), **Heart Chakra** (Anahata), **Throat Chakra** (Vishuddha), **Third-Eye Chakra** (Ajna), and the **Crown Chakra** (Sahasrara).

In this reasoning of my (Christ) teachings; you'll retain clarity of Love to undertake spiritual awakening and enlightenment. Hence, the spiritual awareness of number seventy (enlightenment) relates to the **Universal Law of Spiritual Awakening** times seven (common core chakra).

Our Lord is bringing awareness to the self-control and stability to maintain cohesiveness of inner strength in "being still" for a little while.

KJV Matthew 18: verse 23

Therefore is the kingdom of heaven likened unto a certain king, which would take account of his servants.

Comment appropriately to "Therefore is the kingdom of heaven likened unto a certain king, which would take account of his servants."

Likewise, the kingdom of heaven is our Lord God responsible (account) for those willing to accept (servants) his teaching in the New Commandments.

KJV Matthew 18: verse 24

And when he had begun to reckon, one was brought unto him, which owed him ten thousand talents.

Comment appropriately to "And when he had begun to reckon, one was brought unto him, which owed him ten thousand talents."

Notwithstanding, once he took account of the kingdom, a servant was delivered before he owed ten thousand currencies.

KJV Matthew 18: verse 25

But forasmuch as he had not to pay, his lord commanded him to be sold, and his wife, and children, and all that he had, and payment to be made.

Comment appropriately to "But forasmuch as he had not to pay, his lord commanded him to be sold, and his wife, and children, and all that he had, and payment to be made."

Nonetheless, without conscious thought, the servant reluctantly forgot to repay his master the currencies.

Afterward, his Lord gave the orders to sell all that he owned, including his wife, children, and land, in the effort to repay his debt.

KJV Matthew 18: verse 26

The servant therefore fell down, and worshipped him, saying, Lord, have patience with me, and I will pay thee all.

Comment appropriately to "The servant therefore fell down, and worshipped him, saying, Lord, have patience with me, and I will pay thee all."

Without delay, the servant fell to his knees in response (worshipped) to repentance to his Lord, thus saying. Please be patient with me; please do not take all that I own because I give you my word to repay every currency owed.

KJV Matthew 18: verse 27

Then the lord of that servant was moved with compassion,

and loosed him, and forgave him the debt.

Comment appropriately to "Then the lord of that servant was moved with compassion, and loosed him, and forgave him the debt."

Subsequently, the Lord was moved by the servant's repentance of sins, for the Father moved in the heart with compassion - thus, liberating him from unrighteous thoughts, deeds, and actions.

It essentially forgives him of his wrongdoings.

KJV Matthew 18: verse 28

But the same servant went out, and found one of his fellowservants, which owed him an hundred pence: and he laid hands on him, and took *him* by the throat, saying, Pay me that thou owest.

Comment appropriately to "But the same servant went out, and found one of his fellowservants, which owed him an hundred pence: and he laid hands on him, and took *him* by the throat, saying, Pay me that thou owest."

Accordingly, the same servant of God left feeling out of the presence of his grace found another fellow-servant of the highest.

Despite his inner anger in the subconscious mind (alter ego), he owed him one hundred coinage and placed a strong arm on him. Then, grasping the neck area with verbiage threatening saying, give me what you owe today.

KJV Matthew 18: verse 29

And his fellowservant fell down at his feet, and besought him, saying, Have patience with me, and I will pay thee all.

Comment appropriately to "And his fellowservant fell down at his feet, and besought him, saying, Have patience with me, and I will pay thee all."

Similarly, in the like manner, a fellow servant fell kneeling whaling (a soul's deep sorrow of truths), also asking for repentance for his wrongdoing. Thus, consciously forgetting to repay all debt owed asking for mercy (give or receiving mercy has a payment of Love and Peace).

Note: Our Lord is bringing awareness (light) for the allowances of others to bear forgiveness. Our Father has compassion on us in the same manner.

KJV Matthew 18: verse 30

And he would not: but went and cast him into prison, till he should pay the debt.

Comment appropriately to "And he would not: but went and cast him into prison, till he should pay the debt."

Thus, within the subconscious (alter ego) human mind placed him in the confinement (prison) of bitter anger inwardly until he paid all that the servant owed.

KJV Matthew 18: verse 31

So when his fellowservants saw what was done, they were

very sorry, and came and told unto their lord all that was done.

Comment appropriately to "So when his fellowservants saw what was done, they were very sorry, and came and told unto their lord all that was done."

Therefore, when others (fellow-servants) witnessed these wrongdoings done to their brother in Christ, they were remorseful of these actions. Hence, went inwardly rebuking before heaven (Lord, keeper of knowledge) all which sees all things.

KJV Matthew 18: verse 32

Then his lord, after that he had called him, said unto him, O thou wicked servant, I forgave thee all that debt, because thou desiredst me:

Comment appropriately to "Then his lord, after that he had called him, said unto him, O thou wicked servant, I forgave thee all that debt, because thou desiredst me:"

After that, the Lord in **Universal mind** under the **Universal Law of Balance or Fair Exchange** called upon him and said in effect, your unrighteous servant (wicked servant). Your Lord God has forgiven you of your wrongdoings because of repentance.

(Remember, our God maintains balance throughout his Universe by **Universal Law**, and in this case. Lack of forgiveness in coinage owed towards a fellow servant).

KJV Matthew 18: verse 33

Shouldest not thou also have had compassion on thy fellowservant, even as I had pity on thee?

Comment appropriately to "Shouldest not thou also have had compassion on thy fellowservant, even as I had pity on thee?"

Therefore, how did you not display compassion on your brother (fellow servant) as I showed empathy unto you?

KJV Matthew 18: verse 34

And his lord was wroth, and delivered him to the tormentors, till he should pay all that was due unto him.

Comment appropriately to "And his lord was wroth, and delivered him to the tormentors, till he should pay all that was due unto him."

Even so, in this wrongful doing of the servant, Universal Law (Lord) expressed (wroth) unrighteous actions by Law (tormentor) in the mind until all forgiveness (payment) was due back to the Universe.

Note: The **Universal Law of Honesty** does indeed take effect in repayment leading to Love.

KJV Matthew 18: verse 35

So likewise shall my heavenly Father do also unto you, if ye from your hearts forgive not every one his brother their trespasses.

Comment appropriately to "So likewise shall my heavenly Father do also unto you, if ye from your hearts forgive not every one his brother their trespasses."

So, likewise, if you do not forgive all, our heavenly Father will not forgive you in the same manner.

Matthew Chapter 19

KJV Matthew 19: verse 4

And he answered and said unto them, Have ye not read, that he which made *them* at the beginning made them male and female,

Comment appropriately to "Have ye not read, that he which made *them* at the beginning made them male and female,"

In certainty, scribes wrote from the beginning (Law of Moses) that God our Father created us androgynous (both male and female).

Note: As a spiritual being, and if you accept this truth, we can incarnate of either sex of our choice depending on the karmic lessons we carry.

KJV Matthew 19: verse 5

And said, For this cause shall a man leave father and mother, and shall cleave to his wife: and they twain shall be one flesh?

Comment appropriately to "And said, For this cause shall a man leave father and mother, and shall cleave to his wife: and they twain shall be one flesh?"

Jesus says, and for this reason, a spiritual being leaves the father (Heavenly Father) and mother (heaven) and shall unite (cleave) in the consciousness of mind (Father's mind).

Thus, the body of Christ shall team together in the conscious mind (mother) spiritual body (flesh), including the subconscious mind (twain) as one.

Note: Upon taking an incarnation into physical form, you take on a human mind which uses five senses for survival on the earthly plane. Those five senses are, Sight, Touch, Smell, Taste, and Sound.

KJV Matthew 19: verse 6

Wherefore they are no more twain, but one flesh. What therefore God hath joined together, let not man put asunder.

Comment appropriately to "Wherefore they are no more twain, but one flesh. What therefore God hath joined together, let not man put asunder."

Therefore, they are one flesh in this unity of consciousness, subconscious mind, and spiritual body. Indeed, what the Father has joined together let no man (human being) separate.

KJV Matthew 19: verse 8

He saith unto them, Moses because of the hardness of your

hearts suffered you to put away your wives: but from the beginning it was not so.

Comment appropriately to "He saith unto them, Moses because of the hardness of your hearts suffered you to put away your wives: but from the beginning it was not so."

Jesus said of Moses and the Laws; because of your refusal and inwardly affliction you allowed in your heart was mandated to write such deeds against your wives. Yet, I tell you, this wasn't true initially because this is far from Love.

KJV Matthew 19: verse 9

And I say unto you, Whosoever shall put away his wife, except *it be* for fornication, and shall marry another, committeth adultery: and whoso marrieth her which is put away doth commit adultery.

Comment appropriately to "And I say unto you, Whosoever shall put away his wife, except *it be* for fornication, and shall marry another, committeth adultery: and whoso marrieth her which is put away doth commit adultery."

As for in my New Commandments, whoever disregards his conscious thoughts that come from the Father suffers greatly unless intimacy (fornication) by way of the alter ego (human mind).

Yet, if one takes relations (commits adultery) and marries the mind within oneself, then he has indeed put himself down in an intimate affair.

Note: In essence, you can not commit adultery in mind; you can only commit adultery in the human flesh. However, to counter this point, you can keep unrighteous thoughts leading to sinful deeds in mind causing your soul affliction considering the kingdom.

KJV Matthew 19: verse 11

But he said unto them, All *men* cannot receive this saying, save *they* to whom it is given.

Comment appropriately to "All *men* cannot receive this saying, save *they* to whom it is given"

Considering the kingdom, not all men seek truths or search for righteousness. Those who seek truths of the kingdom share the great news given freely.

KJV Matthew 19: verse 12

For there are some eunuchs, which were so born from *their* mother's womb: and there are some eunuchs, which were made eunuchs of men: and there be eunuchs, which have made themselves eunuchs for the kingdom of heaven's sake. He that is able to receive *it*, let him receive *it*.

Comment appropriately to "For there are some eunuchs, which were so born from *their* mother's womb: and there are some eunuchs, which were made eunuchs of men:"

Contrarily, some mercenaries believe without a doubt that they were born unto a physical mom and dad, and that is life in its entirety.

Comment appropriately to "and there be eunuchs, which have made themselves eunuchs for the kingdom of heaven's sake. He that is able to receive *it*, let him receive *it*."

Nonetheless, some mercenaries have obtained conscious awareness in the kingdom for heaven's sake. Souls capable of understanding and accepting these truths and secrets behind the "Teachings of Jesus Christ."

KJV Matthew 19: verse 14

But Jesus said, Suffer little children, and forbid them not, to come unto me: for of such is the kingdom of heaven.

Comment appropriately to "Suffer little children, and forbid them not, to come unto me: for of such is the kingdom of heaven."

Thus says the Lord, surrender and allow the children of God and do not deny them access to me; for there is the kingdom of heaven.

KJV Matthew 19: verse 17

And he said unto him, Why callest thou me good? *there is* none good but one, *that is*, God: but if thou wilt enter into life, keep the commandments.

Comment appropriately to "Why callest thou me good? *there is* none good but one, *that is,* God: but if thou wilt enter into life, keep the commandments."

Furthermore, how in your spirit do you see truths (me good)? Indeed, there is one greater, God; Thus, if you follow my

New Commandments after that, you shall undoubtedly enter the life of the kingdom.

KJV Matthew 19: verse 18

He saith unto him, Which? Jesus said, Thou shalt do no murder, Thou shalt not commit adultery, Thou shalt not steal, Thou shalt not bear false witness,

Comment appropriately to "Thou shalt do no murder, Thou shalt not commit adultery, Thou shalt not steal, Thou shalt not bear false witness,"

Therefore, you shall not kill, you shall commit lude acts, you shall not take what isn't rightfully yours, and thou shall not lie against thy brother for any reason.

KJV Matthew 19: verse 19

Honour thy father and *thy* mother: and, Thou shalt love thy neighbour as thyself.

Comment appropriately to "Honour thy father and *thy* mother: and, Thou shalt love thy neighbour as thyself."

Finally, honor your Heavenly Father and the consciousness of your mind (Heaven). Furthermore, Love your neighbor as much as you Love yourself in all things.

KJV Matthew 19: verse 21

Jesus said unto him, If thou wilt be perfect, go *and* sell that thou hast, and give to the poor, and thou shalt have treasure in heaven: and come *and* follow me.

Comment appropriately to "If thou wilt be perfect, go *and* sell that thou hast, and give to the poor, and thou shalt have treasure in heaven: *and* come and follow me."

Therefore, seek truths in all things which are of God, and you shall be perfect. Therefore, depart the evil mind (alter ego) with vigor and zest for life, thus giving away those things, not from God's kingdom (give to the poor), i.e., lust, anger, bitterness, sadness, and fear.

Note: These things are not of God and are temporary, lower vibrations.

Furthermore, continue to store up treasures in the consciousness (heaven) and come and accept those things that are valid in my teachings.

KJV Matthew 19: verse 23

Then said Jesus unto his disciples, Verily I say unto you, That a rich man shall hardly enter into the kingdom of heaven.

Comment appropriately to "Verily I say unto you, That a rich man shall hardly enter into the kingdom of heaven."

In all truths for entering the kingdom of heaven, for a man with earthly riches who walks believing he is the body and not the mind. He will indeed no way see the kingdom of heaven.

KJV Matthew 19: verse 24

And again I say unto you, It is easier for a camel to go

through the eye of a needle, than for a rich man to enter into the kingdom of God.

Comment appropriately to "And again I say unto you,"

For it is written again in my New Testament,

Comment appropriately to "It is easier for a camel to go through the eye of a needle, than for a rich man to enter into the kingdom of God."

For this purpose, the camel refers to the animals of the subconscious mind, i.e., (oxen, cattle, camel), thus, slow-moving emotions. Jesus uses this as a ***metaphor*** (*camel through the eye of a needle*).

Therefore, a man with material wealth or earthly riches believing he is the body and not the mind may remain spiritually dead. This is mainly because earthly riches die with the body. Thus, they distract one from searching for true wealth that is spiritual.

KJV Matthew 19: verse 26

But Jesus beheld *them*, and said unto them, With men this is impossible; but with God all things are possible.

Comment appropriately to "With men this is impossible; but with God all things are possible."

Indeed, things are impossible with men physically on this earth plane; however, with God indeed, all things are possible.

KJV Matthew 19: verse 28

And Jesus said unto them, Verily I say unto you, That ye which have followed me, in the regeneration when the Son of man shall sit in the throne of his glory, ye also shall sit upon twelve thrones, judging the twelve tribes of Israel.

Comment appropriately to "Verily I say unto you,"

Listen to these truths of my New Commandments.

Comment appropriately to "That ye which have followed me, in the regeneration when the Son of man shall sit in the throne of his glory, ye also shall sit upon twelve thrones, judging the twelve tribes of Israel."

For my disciples (follow me) shall witness in all my glory where the Son of man shall sit (throne) on the right hand of God the Father. Thus, bringing forth righteous alignment upon all within God's Kingdom (Israel).

Note: The twelve tribes refer to the mind of the conscious Self true desire of his own Dominion, which leads to completion. As far as judging, God the Father, God the Son, and through the Holy Spirit do not judge abate for the mere reason of Love and Truth.

KJV Matthew 19: verse 29

And every one that hath forsaken houses, or brethren, or sisters, or father, or mother, or wife, or children, or lands, for my name's sake, shall receive an hundredfold, and shall inherit everlasting life.

Comment appropriately to "And every one that hath forsaken houses, or brethren, or sisters, or father, or mother, or wife, or children, or lands, for my name's sake, shall receive an hundredfold, and shall inherit everlasting life."

Indeed, for every soul that becomes poor in spirit, denounces earthly brothers, or human flesh sisters, disowns their earthly dad, repudiates their earthly mom, vacates all its children, sell all of their lands for Jesus' namesake.

Shall indeed inherit everlasting life in the Kingdom of God.

KJV Matthew 19: verse 30

But many *that are* first shall be last; and the last *shall be* first.

Comment appropriately to "But many *that are* first shall be last; and the last *shall be* first."

Accordingly, in a prideful boast in the alter ego, the first shall be last, and the humble and meek before God shall be first.

Matthew Chapter 20

KJV Matthew 20: verse 1

For the kingdom of heaven is like unto a man *that is* an householder, which went out early in the morning to hire labourers into his vineyard.

Comment appropriately to "For the kingdom of heaven is like unto a man *that is* an householder, which went out early in the morning to hire labourers into his vineyard."

For this purpose, the kingdom of heaven is the Father in his domain (household) searching for souls (labors) to do the works he sent **all** to do.

Thus, the first part of a soul's day in the cycle of desires leads to enlightenment by morning.

The man (spiritual being) led them to discover all truths by the word of God (vineyard) in the teachings given unto our Lord, Jesus Christ.

KJV Matthew 20: verse 2

And when he had agreed with the labourers for a penny a

day, he sent them into his vineyard.

Comment appropriately to "And when he had agreed with the labourers for a penny a day, he sent them into his vineyard"

Thus, when the soul (labor) agreed to take his incarnation in search of heavenly wealth (penny) in the day (first cycle of a soul's desires). He departed from his image (spiritual body) into a physical body with the word of God (vineyard) within him.

Note: A penny indicates the heavenly wealth of the soul seeking the spiritual wealth of abundance, which indeed transmutes on the earthly plane. However, all earthly riches are not spiritual wealth.

KJV Matthew 20: verse 3

And he went out about the third hour, and saw others standing idle in the marketplace,

Comment appropriately to "And he went out about the third hour, and saw others standing idle in the marketplace,"

The Father again went out in the morning (third hour), still in the same cycle of desire. I noticed others being distracted by material desires (marketplace) of this world, ignoring (idle) their work given by the Father.

KJV Matthew 20: verse 4

And said unto them; Go ye also into the vineyard, and whatsoever is right I will give you. And they went their way.

Comment appropriately to "And said unto them; Go ye also into the vineyard, and whatsoever is right I will give you. And they went their way."

Afterward, our Father says with Love, go with my Son Jesus with my New Commandment, and my word of God (vineyard). Whosoever finds righteousness; I will find favor in the kingdom. So, they all went their own way.

KJV Matthew 20: verse 5

Again he went out about the sixth and ninth hour, and did likewise.

Comment appropriately to "Again he went out about the sixth and ninth hour, and did likewise."

Again, the Father went about the kingdom in the sixth hour (evening), the second cycle of a soul's desire for enlightenment.

Once again, the ninth hour (later in the evening cycle) where the soul's light remains somewhat dim of spiritual knowledge.

KJV Matthew 20: verse 6

And about the eleventh hour he went out, and found others standing idle, and saith unto them, Why stand ye here all the day idle?

Comment appropriately to "And about the eleventh hour he went out, and found others standing idle, and saith unto them, Why stand ye here all the day idle?"

Likewise, the Father went about in the eleventh hour (end of the evening) finding soul's still uselessly wondering about the kingdom (not doing the work the Father gave to each).

Thus, why are you avoiding (idle) the work I gave you that you agreed to do for the kingdom on this earthly plane?

KJV Matthew 20: verse 7

They say unto him, Because no man hath hired us. He saith unto them, Go ye also into the vineyard; and whatsoever is right, *that* shall ye receive.

Comment appropriately to "They say unto him, Because no man hath hired us. He saith unto them, Go ye also into the vineyard; and whatsoever is right, *that* shall ye receive."

The children said unto the Father because no other soul has given us truths of the kingdom for which to share these things which are within us. So, the Father said back to the child, go with the word of God (vineyard) within you and do righteous things for others.

Then, you will receive those things which you do for others with my blessing.

KJV Matthew 20: verse 8

So when even was come, the lord of the vineyard saith unto his steward, Call the labourers, and give them *their* hire, beginning from the last unto the first.

Comment appropriately to "So when even was come, the lord of the vineyard saith unto his steward, Call the labourers, and give them *their* hire, beginning from the last unto the first."

So, when the end of the first cycle (evening) ends, the soul's light remains dim to spiritual knowledge. The Father called upon his glory in the Son, Jesus Christ.

Call ye souls (labor) thus giving unto each its wealth (hire) obtained during its journey on truths onset those with prideful minds (last) to those with humble and meek minds (first).

KJV Matthew 20: verse 9

And when they came that *were hired* about the eleventh hour, they received every man a penny.

Comment appropriately to "And when they came that *were hired* about the eleventh hour, they received every man a penny."

To this end, each soul (hire) labored in the field (subconscious mind) at the end of the first cycle (evening in the eleventh hour). Hence, they received what they each had labored for in spiritual knowledge leading to spiritual wealth (penny).

KJV Matthew 20: verse 10

But when the first came, they supposed that they should have received more; and they likewise received every man a penny.

Comment appropriately to "But when the first came, they

supposed that they should have received more; and they likewise received every man a penny."

However, when the prideful that boasted on earth (first on the earthly plane) came to believe they should receive more spiritual wealth than the last on earth (meek and humble-minded).

The prideful on earth with earthly riches who rule with money that fades with the human body felt they should receive more wealth (penny) in the kingdom than those they *dominated* on the earthly plane.

KJV Matthew 20: verse 11

And when they had received *it*, they murmured against the goodman of the house,

Comment appropriately to "And when they had received *it*, they murmured against the goodman of the house,"

Nonetheless, the prideful on the earthly plane (first) received their spiritual wealth (minimum). The first hired (earthly riches) became troubled (murmured) in the kingdom of heaven before the Father.

KJV Matthew 20: verse 12

Saying, These last have wrought *but* one hour, and thou hast made them equal unto us, which have borne the burden and heat of the day.

Comment appropriately to "Saying, These last have wrought *but* one hour, and thou hast made them equal unto us, which have borne the burden and heat of the day."

Hence, the first hire (earthly riches) said, the meek and humble were last on the earthly plane working minimum (one hour) wherefore I (first hire) worked hard providing jobs for many.

However, you have made them equal in (spiritual wealth) pay, and wherefore we took on headaches (heat of the day) - **Note**: In brief, the **day** includes both morning and evening of a soul's journey to enlightenment.

Lastly, we were tormented in the mind of the earthly burdens doing good for others on earth, yet we still receive equal gains.

KJV Matthew 20: verse 13

But he answered one of them, and said, Friend, I do thee no wrong: didst not thou agree with me for a penny?

Comment appropriately to "But he answered one of them, and said, Friend, I do thee no wrong: didst not thou agree with me for a penny?"

The Father said unto the gentle soul, my child, I, therefore, do no wrong on the works I gave unto you to do. Did you not agree with me to do spiritual works of spiritual wealth (penny) once living upon the earthly plane?

KJV Matthew 20: verse 14

Take *that* thine *is*, and go thy way: I will give unto this last, even as unto thee.

Comment appropriately to "Take *that* thine *is*, and go thy way: I will give unto this last, even as unto thee."

Therefore, accept spiritual truths and continue your journey; thus, I shall give knowledge unto each even as I have given to you.

KJV Matthew 20: verse 15

Is it not lawful for me to do what I will with mine own? Is thine eye evil, because I am good?

Comment appropriately to "Is it not lawful for me to do what I will with mine own? Is thine eye evil, because I am good?"

Indeed, is my kingdom of heaven, not mine to do which I please? Our mind's eye (third eye) with the dim light of truths, aren't I a Good Man?

Note: Jesus uses the Good Man in the context of these parables to indicate the Father in heaven.

KJV Matthew 20: verse 16

So the last shall be first, and the first last: for many be called, but few chosen.

Comment appropriately to "So the last shall be first, and the first last: for many be called, but few chosen."

As a result, the meek and humble (last) shall be first, and the prideful and domineering (first) shall be last; however, so few do enter the kingdom of heaven.

Many of Christ is accepting, so few do the works of the Father.

KJV Matthew 20: verse 18

Behold, we go up to Jerusalem; and the Son of man shall be betrayed unto the chief priests and unto the scribes, and they shall condemn him to death,

Comment appropriately to "Behold, we go up to Jerusalem; and the Son of man shall be betrayed unto the chief priests and unto the scribes,"

For this reason, we must go to the Jerusalem, where the Son of man must be delivered (betrayed) into the unrighteous (chief priest) hands.

To bring forth God's New Commandments (scribes) to come into the world to end all suffering.

Comment appropriately to "and they shall condemn him to death,"

For they (evil doers) will find him guilty (judging) in their court of law of the subconscious mind.

KJV Matthew 20: verse 19

And shall deliver him to the Gentiles to mock, and to scourge, and to crucify *him*: and the third day he shall rise again.

Comment appropriately to "And shall deliver him to the Gentiles to mock, and to scourge, and to crucify *him*: and the third day he shall rise again."

Additionally, they will betray (deliver) him before the unrighteous in mind (Gentiles) to make fun (mock) of him and the *spiritual teachings*.

Thus, afflict (scourge) him verbally with their inward anger, saying, remove his teachings (crucify) that doesn't agree with Moses's Laws.

However, on the third day with celebration and triumph, he shall indeed rise again.

Note: Remember in this passage of scripture that the Messiah is prophesying on his ending. Thus, upon death in the physical, his truths become revealed in his facts of him being God in Trinity of oneness with the Father.

Truly I tell you, no other who has come before Jesus Christ can stand against these truths.

KJV Matthew 20: verse 21

And he said unto her, What wilt thou? She saith unto him, Grant that these my two sons may sit, the one on thy right hand, and the other on the left, in thy kingdom.

Comment appropriately to "What wilt thou?"

For what truths are you seeking that is already within you?

KJV Matthew 20: verse 22

But Jesus answered and said, Ye know not what ye ask. Are ye able to drink of the cup that I shall drink of, and to be baptized with the baptism that I am baptized with? They say unto him, We are able.

Comment appropriately to "Ye know not what ye ask. Are ye able to drink of the cup that I shall drink of,"

Woman, if you genuinely accepted my teachings, you would know that what you ask is not within the truths of the kingdom. Yet are you able to carry the burdens of all souls for righteousness' sake that I have come into the world to do?

Comment appropriately to "and to be baptized with the baptism that I am baptized with? They say unto him, We are able."

Additionally, are you ready to be purified by the Holy Spirit in the renewing of the mind, purity of heart, the righteousness of forgiving in all situations and circumstances from the teachings of God? Are you willing?

KJV Matthew 20: verse 23

And he saith unto them, Ye shall drink indeed of my cup, and be baptized with the baptism that I am baptized with: but to sit on my right hand, and on my left, is not mine to give, but *it shall be given to them* for whom it is prepared of my Father.

Comment appropriately to "Ye shall drink indeed of my cup, and be baptized with the baptism that I am baptized with:"

With certainty, you will indeed baptize (purify the mind) by the Holy Spirit (baptism) with the anointing of spirit through transcendental meditation.

Therefore, to bring about purity of the heart, righteous forgiving in all situations and circumstances comes from God's teachings.

Comment appropriately to "but to sit on my right hand, and on my left, is not mine to give, but *it shall be given to them* for whom it is prepared of my Father."

However, to be (state of mind) righteous (right hand) or not to be (unsure in mind) unrighteous is for the soul seeking enlightenment through my teachings which is a choice of "Free Will."

Indeed, our Lord Jesus Christ shall give it for those who genuinely seek the kingdom of the Father. In addition, it is given to those who it is prepared for as Chosen elects.

KJV Matthew 20: verse 25

But Jesus called them *unto him*, and said, Ye know that the princes of the Gentiles exercise dominion over them, and they that are great exercise authority upon them.

Comment appropriately to "Ye know that the princes of the Gentiles exercise dominion over them, and they that are great exercise authority upon them."

So, if you are aware of the alter ego (human mind), which portrays both good and evil reasons (princes of the Gentile). Then indeed, you should become more aware of the evil which grows when unattended with spiritual truths.

KJV Matthew 20: verse 26

But it shall not be so among you: but whosoever will be great among you, let him be your minister;

Comment appropriately to "But it shall not be so among you: but whosoever will be great among you, let him be your minister;"

Therefore, if there is one amongst you who understands these truths, let him know where these truths hold agreement.

KJV Matthew 20: verse 27

And whosoever will be chief among you, let him be your servant:

Comment appropriately to "And whosoever will be chief among you, let him be your servant:"

Also, if there is one with clear understanding (chief), let him indeed be your servant with Love.

KJV Matthew 20: verse 28

Even as the Son of man came not to be ministered unto, but to minister, and to give his life a ransom for many.

Comment appropriately to "Even as the Son of man came not to be ministered unto, but to minister, and to give his life a ransom for many."

Even as the Lord thy God came into being to provide wisdom and guidance to his flock, he also gave himself (ransom) to all in the teachings for all a reason to enter God's Kingdom.

KJV Matthew 20: verse 32

And Jesus stood still, and called them, and said, What will ye that I shall do unto you?

Comment appropriately to "What will ye that I shall do unto you?"

In other words, what miracle blessing do you believe I will do for you?

Matthew Chapter 21

KJV Matthew 21: verse 2

Saying unto them, Go into the village over against you, and straightway ye shall find an ass tied, and a colt with her: loose *them*, and bring *them* unto me.

Comment appropriately to "Go into the village over against you, and straightway ye shall find an ass tied, and a colt with her: loose *them*, and bring *them* unto me."

Accordingly, go within the subconscious mind (village) of the altered ego human mind (against you), do not deviate away from the path (straightway) of righteousness while in solitude (meditation).

Once on the path, you will find emotions (donkey and colt); hence, animals refer to slow-moving emotions. Thus, old lingering emotions are negative (fear, doubt, and worry) in the field of the subconscious mind.

Loosen them and bring them to me in prayer and transcendental meditation.

KJV Matthew 21: verse 3

And if any *man* say ought unto you, ye shall say, The Lord hath need of them; and straightway he will send them.

Comment appropriately to "And if any *man* say ought unto you, ye shall say, The Lord hath need of them; and straightway he will send them."

Therefore, if any soul shall question the Lord's way of worship in the teachings, say to him, my Lord and Savior command these things of me.

Then remain in my peace and on the righteous path (straightway) because the Lord will indeed send them in spirit.

KJV Matthew 21: verse 13

And said unto them, It is written, My house shall be called the house of prayer; but ye have made it a den of thieves.

Comment appropriately to "it is written"

For it was written in the First Testament even before my New Commandments.

Comment appropriately to "My house shall be called the house of prayer; but ye have made it a den of thieves."

God shall call my soul (house) the spirit of worship for thy kingdom; hence, in the haste of wrongful doings (den), you have made it unrighteous because of others (thieves) to lead thee in these acts.

KJV Matthew 21: verse 16

And said unto him, Hearest thou what these say? And Jesus saith unto them, Yea; have ye never read, Out of the mouth of babes and sucklings thou hast perfected praise?

Comment appropriately to "Yea; have ye never read, Out of the mouth of babes and sucklings thou hast perfected praise?"

Jesus said for it was written in the old times, rejoicing from those who enter God's Kingdom because they are perfect children continuously seeking righteousness.

KJV Matthew 21: verse 19

And when he saw a fig tree in the way, he came to it, and found nothing thereon, but leaves only, and said unto it, Let no fruit grow on thee henceforward for ever. And presently the fig tree withered away.

Comment appropriately to "Let no fruit grow on thee henceforward for ever."

Thus says the Lord, allow no teachings outside of Love and truth to grow forever!

KJV Matthew 21: verse 21

Jesus answered and said unto them, Verily I say unto you, If ye have faith, and doubt not, ye shall not only do this *which is done* to the fig tree, but also if ye shall say unto this mountain, Be thou removed, and be thou cast into the sea; it shall be done.

Comment appropriately to "Verily I say unto you,"

Truly I give this truth for entering into the kingdom of heaven.

Comment appropriately to "If ye have faith, and doubt not, ye shall not only do this *which is done* to the fig tree, but also if ye shall say unto this mountain, Be thou removed, and be thou cast into the sea; it shall be done."

If you can believe a thought (picture or image) that flashes in the subconscious mind and hold it (faith), and therefore has this picture in mind and believe that it is true right at this moment (doubt not).

Note: Ever hear the saying a picture is worth a thousand words? Wherefore truthful in mind.

Again, at this moment, how do you feel in the image you are holding in thought? How would it feel if this is true in the heart of this image? (Place feelings behind this image)

Do this as often as you like for truths to hold in the subconscious mind needing to reach consciousness in the Father (heaven).

Then you will not live as the fig tree (empty of truths) because your mindset will be (state of being) accepting this as truth from the Father - hence, a gift from God.

Therefore, allowing that which is beyond your minuscule power to overcome any situation or circumstance (mountain) with Love within Jesus Christ's power.

You shall indeed tell that obstacle to move away - thus casting it by allowing Christ in the subconscious mind to take it away by therefore allowing spirit to proceed by finishing it to its will, which is Love.

KJV Matthew 21: verse 22

And all things, whatsoever ye shall ask in prayer, believing, ye shall receive.

Comment appropriately to "And all things, whatsoever ye shall ask in prayer, believing, ye shall receive"

Therefore, all things (material or spiritual) you ask straightway without hidden motives, you shall indeed receive.

KJV Matthew 21: verse 24

And Jesus answered and said unto them, I also will ask you one thing, which if ye tell me, I in like wise will tell you by what authority I do these things.

Comment appropriately to "I also will ask you one thing, which if ye tell me, I in like wise will tell you by what authority I do these things."

Therefore, I will ask you one thing concerning John the Baptist and if you can reveal its truth. Then, I will present facts about the Kingdom of God.

KJV Matthew 21: verse 25

The baptism of John, whence was it? from heaven, or of

men? And they reasoned with themselves, saying, If we shall say, From heaven; he will say unto us, Why did ye not then believe him?

Comment appropriately to "The baptism of John, whence was it? from heaven, or of men?"

Very well, where did the purification of John the Baptist originate from, heaven or by men?

KJV Matthew 21: verse 27

And they answered Jesus, and said, We cannot tell. And he said unto them, Neither tell I you by what authority I do these things.

Comment appropriately to "Neither tell I you by what authority I do these things."

Nor do I tell you facts about the Kingdom of God.

KJV Matthew 21: verse 28

But what think ye? A *certain* man had two sons; and he came to the first, and said, Son, go work to day in my vineyard.

Comment appropriately to "But what think ye? A *certain* man had two sons; and he came to the first, and said, Son, go work to day in my vineyard."

How do you think it concerns the kingdom of heaven? The Good Man (Our Heavenly Father) approached a couple of his children in heaven and said to the first.

Child, go forth into the world with my Word and spread the good news of the gospels how to enter my kingdom.

Note: Indeed, this reflects a soul taking its incarnation to Gaia, planet earth, to complete its purpose of desire reaching enlightenment.

KJV Matthew 21: verse 29

He answered and said, I will not: but afterward he repented, and went.

Comment appropriately to "He answered and said, I will not: but afterward he repented, and went."

Thus, the child responded with dismay and said, please, Father, not this time. However, later, he did repent and went with Love in his heart.

KJV Matthew 21: verse 30

And he came to the second, and said likewise. And he answered and said, I *go*, sir: and went not.

Comment appropriately to "And he came to the second, and said likewise. And he answered and said, I *go*, sir: and went not."

Likewise, the Father approached the second child again, sending the child into the world with great news.

In the same way, he responded and said, I will go at once, Father; however, he did not go into the world to spread the gospels of the Lord to the end of all suffering.

KJV Matthew 21: verse 31

Whether of them twain did the will of *his* father? They say unto him, The first. Jesus saith unto them, Verily I say unto you, That the publicans and the harlots go into the kingdom of God before you.

Comment appropriately to "Whether of them twain did the will of *his* father?"

So, I ask you, which one of the children did the will of our Father?

Comment appropriately to "Verily I say unto you, That the publicans and the harlots go into the kingdom of God before you."

Therefore, I give these truths for entering the kingdom of heaven. Those who repent before the Father indeed shall enter the kingdom of heaven before those of unrighteousness.

KJV Matthew 21: verse 32

For John came unto you in the way of righteousness, and ye believed him not: but the publicans and the harlots believed him: and ye, when ye had seen *it*, repented not afterward, that ye might believe him.

Comment appropriately to "For John came unto you in the way of righteousness, and ye believed him not: but the publicans and the harlots believed him: and ye, when ye had seen *it*, repented not afterward, that ye might believe him."

Furthermore, the righteous John the Baptist came before the Messiah, and yet you did not believe in him. Yet, there were public servants and fallen women who felt his message and repented.

However, you received his message within consciousness and have yet to acknowledge the Son of Man, nor repented.

KJV Matthew 21: verse 33

Hear another parable: There was a certain householder, which planted a vineyard, and hedged it round about, and digged a winepress in it, and built a tower, and let it out to husbandmen, and went into a far country:

Comment appropriately to "Hear another parable: There was a certain householder, which planted a vineyard, and hedged it round about, and digged a winepress in it,"

Equally important, here's more wisdom upon entering the kingdom: Our Lord brought forth new teachings (vineyard) in the New Commandments in all his knowledge.

He went about teaching to many nations (roundabout) and rooted out (dug) old forms of traditions, worships, and unrighteous instructions on this journey.

Comment appropriately to "and built a tower, and let it out to husbandmen, and went into a far country:"

Thus, building strong stances (tower) for righteousness in the sight of those outside Christianity accepting the teachings in foreign lands. His followers were in control of the vineyard.

KJV Matthew 21: verse 34

And when the time of the fruit drew near, he sent his servants to the husbandmen, that they might receive the fruits of it.

Comment appropriately to "And when the time of the fruit drew near, he sent his servants to the husbandmen, that they might receive the fruits of it."

Conversely, when the day the gospels of spiritual truths were near, God the Father sent out his farmhand (servant) unto the followers (husbandmen) of Jesus for each one to receive more knowledge of the kingdom.

KJV Matthew 21: verse 35

And the husbandmen took his servants, and beat one, and killed another, and stoned another.

Comment appropriately to "And the husbandmen took his servants, and beat one, and killed another, and stoned another."

Consequently, the unrighteous holy men (husbandmen) sent out likewise the inner court and attacked (beat one) the farmhand of his way of worship. Then the inner court assassinates (killed) another farmhand in the subconscious mind by removing him from their sight.

Lastly, they (inner court) insulted (stoned) another farmhand of our Lord God.

KJV Matthew 21: verse 36

Again, he sent other servants more than the first: and they did unto them likewise.

Comment appropriately to "Again, he sent other servants more than the first: and they did unto them likewise."

Once again, the Father sent more farmhands into the field; in fact, they all had obtained more wisdom than before. Unfortunately, however, they too suffered the same as the others likewise.

KJV Matthew 21: verse 37

But last of all he sent unto them his son, saying, They will reverence my son.

Comment appropriately to "But last of all he sent unto them his son, saying, They will reverence my son."

Impressive enough, the Father sent into the world his only Son, thus saying, for sure they will honor my only begotten Son.

KJV Matthew 21: verse 38

But when the husbandmen saw the son, they said among themselves, This is the heir; come, let us kill him, and let us seize on his inheritance.

Comment appropriately to "But when the husbandmen saw the son, they said among themselves, This is the heir; come, let us kill him, and let us seize on his inheritance."

Nevertheless, at first, they (husbandmen) did not recognize the Son. Then, however, the unrighteous holy men, later realizing with amazement, said unto his inner court.

For most excellent is the Son of the Living God; let's crucify and take away what is written concerning him and keep for ourselves (inheritance).

KJV Matthew 21: verse 39

And they caught him, and cast *him* out of the vineyard, and slew *him*.

Comment appropriately to "And they caught him, and cast *him* out of the vineyard, and slew *him*."

Indeed, they took him, cast out his teachings (vineyard), and crucified Him.

KJV Matthew 21: verse 40

When the lord therefore of the vineyard cometh, what will he do unto those husbandmen?

Comment appropriately to "When the lord therefore of the vineyard cometh, what will he do unto those husbandmen?"

He is going forth, likewise when thy Lord comes with the Word of God in righteous thinking. What shall he seek out to get from that holy men and inner court?

KJV Matthew 21: verse 42

Jesus saith unto them, Did ye never read in the scriptures,

The stone which the builders rejected, the same is become the head of the corner: this is the Lord's doing, and it is marvellous in our eyes?

Comment appropriately to "Did ye never read in the scriptures,"

Wherefore, is it not written in the Old Testament for those instructing the Laws of Moses?

Comment appropriately to "The stone which the builders rejected, the same is become the head of the corner: this is the Lord's doing, and it is marvellous in our eyes?"

Alias, the significant number of insults (stone) which the Pharisees (interprets of Religious Laws) and Sadducees (officiated as High Priest) all rejected the truths of Jesus being the Messiah.

Before long, the Lord thy God is indeed doing a marvelous thing right before our eyes!

KJV Matthew 21: verse 43

Therefore say I unto you, The kingdom of God shall be taken from you, and given to a nation bringing forth the fruits thereof.

Comment appropriately to "Therefore say I unto you, The kingdom of God shall be taken from you, and given to a nation bringing forth the fruits thereof."

I (Jesus) give you these new commandments first, genuinely

seek the kingdom of God with all your strength within you. Next, in this manner, the Father shall reserve the domain for those who genuinely seek it within their heart, soul, and mind.

KJV Matthew 21: verse 44

And whosoever shall fall on this stone shall be broken: but on whomsoever it shall fall, it will grind him to powder.

Comment appropriately to "And whosoever shall fall on this stone shall be broken: but on whomsoever it shall fall, it will grind him to powder."

Likewise, whoever shall fall on thy Lord Jesus (stone) shall indeed humble (broken) themselves, and whoever it shall fall upon will certainly cleanse his spirit to righteousness, knowledge, and understanding (powder).

Matthew Chapter 22

KJV Matthew 22: verse 2

The kingdom of heaven is like unto a certain king, which made a marriage for his son,

Comment appropriately to "The kingdom of heaven is like unto a certain king, which made a marriage for his son,"

Indeed, the kingdom of heaven is like our Heavenly Father, which gave its Son a mind being of consciousness.

KJV Matthew 22: verse 3

And sent forth his servants to call them that were bidden to the wedding: and they would not come.

Comment appropriately to "And sent forth his servants to call them that were bidden to the wedding: and they would not come."

Therefore, he sent the followers of Jesus (servants) to come into his wisdom and understanding to life (wedding); however, they neglected spiritual truths because of deceitfulness of this world.

They neglected spiritual works and believed they were indeed the body and not a spiritual being full of resurrection power within itself.

KJV Matthew 22: verse 4

Again, he sent forth other servants, saying, Tell them which are bidden, Behold, I have prepared my dinner: my oxen and *my* fatlings *are* killed, and all things *are* ready: come unto the marriage.

Comment appropriately to "Again, he sent forth other servants, saying, Tell them which are bidden, Behold, I have prepared my dinner: my oxen and *my* fatlings *are* killed,"

Meanwhile, our Lord sent out more followers in Christ into the world who are searching for truths (bidden); indeed, I thy Lord have prepared eternal life (dinner) in consciousness to share knowledge (oxen) and wisdom (fatling) which shall never die.

Comment appropriately to "and all things *are* ready: come unto the marriage."

To this end, all things with the kingdom of heaven are before you, come, accept our oneness (marriage) in the Father.

Note: Purity of the mind produces righteous thinking, and this case. Marriage in mind brings about Love and truth in consciousness.

KJV Matthew 22: verse 5

But they made light of *it*, and went their ways, one to his farm, another to his merchandise:

Comment appropriately to "But they made light of *it*, and went their ways, one to his farm, another to his merchandise:"

Nonetheless, the followers of our Lord and Savior did not hear his voice of righteous acceptance to enter the kingdom.

Thus, they went back to what they have always believed in their minds (farm), thinking they must seek earthly riches (merchandise).

KJV Matthew 22: verse 6

And the remnant took his servants, and entreated *them* spitefully, and slew *them*.

Comment appropriately to "And the remnant took his servants, and entreated *them* spitefully, and slew *them*."

Evildoers were allowed to overcome the alter ego (human mind) of each servant to unrighteous thinking; thus, fornication (spitefully) of the mind left them empty of truths and spiritually dead (slew them).

KJV Matthew 22: verse 7

But when the king heard *thereof,* he was wroth: and he sent forth his armies, and destroyed those murderers, and burned up their city.

Comment appropriately to "But when the king heard *thereof,* he was wroth: and he sent forth his armies, and destroyed those murderers, and burned up their city."

However, when the Father overheard what he knew was happening in the kingdom of Love, he became more compassionate (wroth).

He sent forth more angels (armies) without delay, placing all misdeeds and untruths away in the subconscious mind. Essentially, tormenting all unrighteousness in the alter ego human mind in their presence (city).

KJV Matthew 22: verse 8

Then saith he to his servants, The wedding is ready, but they which were bidden were not worthy.

Comment appropriately to "Then saith he to his servants, The wedding is ready, but they which were bidden were not worthy."

Hence, the Father sent his angels (servants) to purify the subconscious mind with abundant Love and peace. However, few were ready (worthy) from doing the works of the Lord to enter the kingdom of God.

KJV Matthew 22: verse 9

Go ye therefore into the highways, and as many as ye shall find, bid to the marriage.

Comment appropriately to "Go ye therefore into the highways, and as many as ye shall find, bid to the marriage."

Therefore, I go to foreign lands (highways) and mountains,

searching for hearts willing to accept (many as ye shall find) my manifestation of Love and truths (marriage) for peace of mind.

KJV Matthew 22: verse 10

So those servants went out into the highways, and gathered together all as many as they found, both bad and good: and the wedding was furnished with guests.

Comment appropriately to "So those servants went out into the highways, and gathered together all as many as they found, both bad and good: and the wedding was furnished with guests."

Despite followers of Christ avoiding doing the work required to enter God's Kingdom; hence, the Lord sent out his angels into all the world, attracting all walks of faiths (Muslim, Hinduism, Buddhism, Islam, No religion, Folk religions, Sikhism, and Judaism).

Thy Lord God has offered Love and truths with an open heart (furnished) to receive his blessings.

KJV Matthew 22: verse 11

And when the king came in to see the guests, he saw there a man which had not on a wedding garment:

Comment appropriately to "And when the king came in to see the guests, he saw there a man which had not on a wedding garment:"

Thus, when the Lord (king) saw the attendees (guests) who

desired to enter the kingdom of heaven. A soul was pretending to wear an outer appearance of Love and truth (wedding garment).

KJV Matthew 22: verse 12

And he saith unto him, Friend, how camest thou in hither not having a wedding garment? And he was speechless.

Comment appropriately to "And he saith unto him, Friend, how camest thou in hither not having a wedding garment? And he was speechless."

Thus, the Lord said unto the gentle soul, servant, do you not understand the Son of Man sees what is in the heart which is untruthful (garment).

Indeed, the gentle spirit knew this truth inwardly and could not discern truths upon the New Commandments of teachings.

KJV Matthew 22: verse 13

Then said the king to the servants, Bind him hand and foot, and take him away, and cast *him* into outer darkness; there shall be weeping and gnashing of teeth.

Comment appropriately to "Then said the king to the servants, Bind him hand and foot, and take him away, and cast *him* into outer darkness;"

Furthermore, the Lord said unto his servants, constrain this soul heart (hand) while on his journey (foot) to righteousness. Moreover, send him into the world (darkness) to do the works the Father assigned him to do.

Comment appropriately to "there shall be weeping and gnashing of teeth."

Indeed, by not doing the works given by the Father. There will be deep sorrow (weeping) within the soul and confession of true repentance (gnashing of teeth) before God in Heaven.

KJV Matthew 22: verse 14

For many are called, but few *are* chosen.

Comment appropriately to "For many are called, but few *are* chosen."

Many of Christ is accepting, so few (chosen) do the works of the Father.

KJV Matthew 22: verse 18

But Jesus perceived their wickedness, and said, Why tempt ye me, *ye* hypocrites?

Comment appropriately to "Why tempt ye me, *ye* hypocrites?

Thus tells the Lord, why are you troubling me in thy mind, you tricksters.

KJV Matthew 22: verse 19

Shew me the tribute money. And they brought unto him a penny.

Comment appropriately to "Shew me the tribute money."

Indeed, reflect thy value of spiritual worth in relevance to the kingdom of heaven.

KJV Matthew 22: verse 20

And he saith unto them, Whose is this image and superscription?

Comment appropriately to "Whose is this image and superscription?"

Wherefore, does it place value on our Heavenly Father?

KJV Matthew 22: verse 21

They say unto him, Caesar's. Then saith he unto them, Render therefore unto Caesar the things which are Caesar's; and unto God the things that are God's.

Comment appropriately to "Then saith he unto them, Render therefore unto Caesar the things which are Caesar's; and unto God the things that are God's."

Jesus said to them, give Caesar his earthly riches which hold no value in the kingdom of heaven; and give unto God your soul, mind, and spiritual body that belongs to the kingdom of heaven of true wealth.

KJV Matthew 22: verse 29

Jesus answered and said unto them, Ye do err, not knowing the scriptures, nor the power of God.

Comment appropriately to "Ye do err, not knowing the scriptures, nor the power of God."

Consequently, you do not interpret the scriptures correctly. In addition, you do not perceive the power of God.

KJV Matthew 22: verse 30

For in the resurrection they neither marry, nor are given in marriage, but are as the angels of God in heaven.

Comment appropriately to "For in the resurrection they neither marry, nor are given in marriage, but are as the angels of God in heaven."

Indeed, in the renewing (resurrection) of the mind being rebirth, the reason is of one consciousness.

Therefore, it cannot be married or remarried because a spirit (angel) has its own conscious mind in oneness that belongs to God in heaven.

KJV Matthew 22: verse 31

But as touching the resurrection of the dead, have ye not read that which was spoken unto you by God, saying,

Comment appropriately to "But as touching the resurrection of the dead, have ye not read that which was spoken unto you by God, saying,"

Nonetheless, by joining (touching) the altered ego (spiritually dead human mind) in the subconscious mind, have you not understood what our Father said concerning these things?

KJV Matthew 22: verse 32

I am the God of Abraham, and the God of Isaac, and the God of Jacob? God is not the God of the dead, but of the living.

Comment appropriately to "I am the God of Abraham, and the God of Isaac, and the God of Jacob?"

Indeed, I am the God of Abraham, Isaac, and Jacob.

Comment appropriately to "God is not the God of the dead, but of the living."

Therefore, I am not the God of the spiritually dead, only the consciously awakened in mind.

KJV Matthew 22: verse 37

Jesus said unto him, Thou shalt love the Lord thy God with all thy heart, and with all thy soul, and with all thy mind.

Comment appropriately to "Thou shalt love the Lord thy God with all thy heart, and with all thy soul, and with all thy mind."

Thus, saith the Lord, honor your Heavenly Father with all thy might (heart), all thyself (soul), and all thy consciousness.

KJV Matthew 22: verse 38

This is the first and great commandment.

Comment appropriately to "This is the first and great commandment."

Above all, do this continuously in the heart, soul, and mind.

Note: This is the first of the new commandments and the first Universal Law which is to Love.

KJV Matthew 22: verse 39

And the second is like unto it, Thou shalt love thy neighbour as thyself.

Comment appropriately to "And the second is like unto it, Thou shalt love thy neighbour as thyself."

To this end, my first Commandment is like the second. Always, Love your brothers and sisters as much as you Love yourself.

Note: This is the second of the new commandments and the first Universal Law which is to Unconditional Love.

KJV Matthew 22: verse 40

On these two commandments hang all the law and the prophets.

Comment appropriately to "On these two commandments hang all the law and the prophets."

For this purpose, my two commandments are righteous for those to enter God's kingdom.

In addition, these two commandments are present before the

beginning of days in heaven.

Note: These two laws provides segway to the third of the new commandments and the third Universal Law of Oneness.

KJV Matthew 22: verse 42

Saying, What think ye of Christ? whose son is he? They say unto him, *The Son* of David.

Comment appropriately to "What think ye of Christ? whose son is he?"

Therefore, who is Christ? Do you believe in him as the Son of the Highest?

KJV Mathew 22: verse 43

He saith unto them, How then doth David in spirit call him Lord, saying,

Comment appropriately to "How then doth David in spirit call him Lord, saying,"

How did David believeth in him (God) otherwise calling upon the Lord God saying?

KJV Matthew 22: verse 44

The LORD said unto my Lord, Sit thou on my right hand, till I make thine enemies thy footstool?

Comment appropriately to "The LORD said unto my Lord, Sit thou on my right hand, till I make thine enemies thy footstool?"

Thou Servant (David) saith unto my LORD, place eternal Love in my heart (right hand) until all my minds is undivided (enemies) as the evil one. In the stillness of consciousness <u>subduing this journey</u> (footstool).

Note: For this reason, the (right hand) always refers to the heart in your spiritual body; thus, David is consciously acknowledging the mighty hand (heart) and Love of our Lord that gives us strength in the oneness of spirit.

KJV Matthew 22: verse 45

If David then call him Lord, how is he his son?

Comment appropriately to "If David then call him Lord, how is he his son?"

Therefore, if David calls upon thy Lord in consciousness, then for sure the Son is thy God, isn't it so?

Special Note: In addition, our Lord and Savior bring awareness into his Love in the Kingdom of God in the oneness of the Father.

Matthew Chapter 23

KJV Matthew 23: verse 2

Saying, The scribes and the Pharisees sit in Moses' seat:

Comment appropriately to "The scribes and the Pharisees sit in Moses' seat:"

Accordingly, the transcribers that write the Laws in the First Testament and the impostors portraying holy men sit in the best seat in the house of worship and official functions.

Note: Jesus is bringing awareness of how the Laws transgress against the children of God and leads to destruction in consciousness.

KJV Matthew 23: verse 3

All therefore whatsoever they bid you observe, *that* observe and do; but do not ye after their works: for they say, and do not.

Comment appropriately to "All therefore whatsoever they bid you observe, *that* observe and do;"

Consequently, these deceivers do whatever they so choose and forbid you to say anything against their rules.

Comment appropriately to "but do not ye after their works: for they say, and do not."

They instruct others to obey the Laws and orders placed over the followers, and yet, they do not follow these same rules or guidelines.

KJV Matthew 23: verse 4

For they bind heavy burdens and grievous to be borne, and lay *them* on men's shoulders; but they *themselves* will not move them with one of their fingers.

Comment appropriately to "For they bind heavy burdens and grievous to be borne, and lay *them* on men's shoulders; but they *themselves* will not move them with one of their fingers."

Otherwise, they place strict rules which limit the expansion of consciousness (bind heavy burdens) in which they place restrictions (grievous to be borne) that are unfavorable on the shoulders of its followers.

In addition, these stupid rules don't place Love for one another because it favors only those wearing robes and making business (not moving a finger) decisions for the ministry.

KJV Matthew 23: verse 5

But all their works they do for to be seen of men: they make broad their phylacteries, and enlarge the borders of their garments,

Comment appropriately to "But all their works they do for to be seen of men: they make broad their phylacteries, and enlarge the borders of their garments,"

Consequently, they display many heroics in holy places where to be seen as necessary amongst men with flashy robes and sometimes hats with rankings of influences.

KJV Matthew 23: verse 6

And love the uppermost rooms at feasts, and the chief seats in the synagogues,

Comment appropriately to "And love the uppermost rooms at feasts, and the chief seats in the synagogues,"

Furthermore, they revel in lavish banquet halls invited to festivities (feasts) for free; additionally, they have no intentions on compensation to reserve the best seats in the house of worship and sanctuaries.

KJV Matthew 23: verse 7

And greetings in the markets, and to be called of men, Rabbi, Rabbi.

Comment appropriately to "And greetings in the markets, and to be called of men, Rabbi, Rabbi."

So that, they are high in society in the town when followers greet them with the priest, dear leader.

KJV Matthew 23: verse 8

But be not ye called Rabbi: for one is your Master, *even* Christ; and all ye are brethren.

Comment appropriately to "But be not ye called Rabbi: for one is your Master, *even* Christ; and all ye are brethren."

Indeed, be not deceived by calling them teachers (Rabbi) because you only have one teacher, Christ; therefore, you are all my brethren.

KJV Matthew 23: verse 9

And call no *man* your father upon the earth: for one is your Father, which is in heaven.

Comment appropriately to "And call no *man* your father upon the earth: for one is your Father, which is in heaven."

Consequently, call ***no one*** upon the face of the earth under no condition "**FATHER**" because you have "One Father, which is in consciousness" (heaven).

Note: Jesus is bringing awareness of how to enter the kingdom of heaven. Yes, we must remove the notion that our biological parents are only our natural parents during this physical cycle of evolution. Also, this authoritarian position should include all forms of titles, formal and informal.

In addition, we should call everyone upon the face of Gaia (Mother Earth) by their God-given name at birth. Each name at birth was carefully assembled prior to incarnation in heaven as each person's name has spiritual implications and meaning.

Not to mention, our God opposes titles to place men above one another when indeed we are its children in his heart.

So, from this point forward, do not call anyone regardless of title: Teacher, Doctor, Minister, Father, Priest, Pastor, Attorney, and even a Judge. Indeed, we all are one in God and should remove bias restrictions of titles.

The Lord, thy God, will ensure Universal laws and principles adhered to Love and Peace.

KJV Matthew 23: verse 10

Neither be ye called masters: for one is your Master, *even* Christ.

Comment appropriately to "Neither be ye called masters: for one is your Master, *even* Christ."

Therefore, do not be called master or call others master because you have one Master: Christ.

KJV Matthew 23: verse 11

But he that is greatest among you shall be your servant.

Comment appropriately to "But he that is greatest among you shall be your servant."

Indeed, whoever is the humblest with spiritual awareness shall serve his brothers in spiritual conversations.

In other words, the one who has obtained higher learning

shall help others in assistance on their journey.

KJV Matthew 23: verse 12

And whosoever shall exalt himself shall be abased; and he that shall humble himself shall be exalted.

Comment appropriately to "And whosoever shall exalt himself shall be abased; and he that shall humble himself shall be exalted."

Forever, whoever boasts before many shall remain in the darkness of the kingdom; nonetheless, the one who is modest with Love shall be first in the kingdom full of light for all in the Father.

KJV Matthew 23: verse 13

But woe unto you, scribes and Pharisees, hypocrites! for ye shut up the kingdom of heaven against men: for ye neither go in *yourselves*, neither suffer ye them that are entering to go in.

Comment appropriately to "But woe unto you, scribes and Pharisees, hypocrites! for ye shut up the kingdom of heaven against men: "

Therefore, misery to you, men of the cloth you deceivers (scribes and Pharisees). Consequently, you do not allow your followers to enter the kingdom of heaven, not to mention you are against souls who dare question you!

Comment appropriately to "for ye neither go in *yourselves*, neither suffer ye them that are entering to go in."

Furthermore, you do not know how to enter the kingdom of God yourselves, so, therefore, you suffer my sheep (followers) not to understand how to or where to begin.

KJV Matthew 23: verse 14

Woe unto you, scribes and Pharisees, hypocrites! for ye devour widows' houses, and for a pretence make long prayer: therefore ye shall receive the greater damnation.

Comment appropriately to "Woe unto you, scribes and Pharisees, hypocrites! for ye devour widows' houses, and for a pretence make long prayer."

Once again, misery to you, you men of the cloth, you deceivers (scribes and Pharisees). For this reason, you leave a soul (widows' house) empty to unrighteous (pretence), believing in your devilish human-mind with your babbling and gibberish prayers.

Comment appropriately to: "therefore ye shall receive the greater damnation."

For these wrongful deeds (receiving tithes), you shall indeed receive most darkness (greater damnation) in your unpredictable ways.

Note: The Messiah is bringing awareness to those receiving favor from its members (men) by not earning their wages through spirit. This wrongful violation of the Universal Law of Invocation presence an implication of karmic debt earned.

You are wrongfully taking what isn't rightfully earned.

KJV Matthew 23: verse 15

Woe unto you, scribes and Pharisees, hypocrites! for ye compass sea and land to make one proselyte, and when he is made, ye make him twofold more the child of hell than yourselves.

Comment appropriately to "Woe unto you, scribes and Pharisees, hypocrites! for ye compass sea and land to make one proselyte, and when he is made, ye make him twofold more the child of hell than yourselves."

Even again, misery to you, you men of the cloth, (scribes and Pharisees) you deceivers (hypocrites).

Accordingly, you are without knowledge of the inner workings of the subconscious mind, for the emotions (sea) and the internal planting (land) of fruitful understanding to become followers of Christ as a disciple (proselyte).

Therefore, with your unrighteous and untruthful doctrine (twofold), you lead a child of God to lies within the subconscious mind just like yourselves.

KJV Matthew 23: verse 16

Woe unto you, *ye* blind guides, which say, Whosoever shall swear by the temple, it is nothing; but whosoever shall swear by the gold of the temple, he is a debtor!

Comment appropriately to "Woe unto you, *ye* blind guides, which say, Whosoever shall swear by the temple, it is nothing; but whosoever shall swear by the gold of the temple, he is a debtor!"

Misery and anguish unto you, for you, are not worthy (blind guides) of instructing my New Commandments; thus, you tell those affirm by the existence. Therefore, it is useless because it is from the evil one (human mind).

However, you tell those to affirm the physical material building called the cathedral; he is in God's grace paying tithings.

Note: Our Lord continues to bring awareness in the business dealings of evildoers accepting sums of money. Beware, because tithing does not by any way assure you are entering the kingdom of heaven. (Not even one penny)

KJV Matthew 23: verse 17

Ye fools and blind: for whether is greater, the gold, or the temple that sanctifieth the gold?

Comment appropriately to "*Ye* fools and blind: for whether is greater, the gold, or the temple that sanctifieth the gold?"

Moreover, you deceivers and con artists: explain, which is more profitable, the illusion of earthly riches, or the misuse of the place of worship tithing to gain material riches?

KJV Matthew 23: verse 18

And, Whosoever shall swear by the altar, it is nothing; but whosoever sweareth by the gift that is upon it, he is guilty.

Comment appropriately to "And, Whosoever shall swear

by the altar, it is nothing; but whosoever sweareth by the gift that is upon it, he is guilty."

To this end, whoever declares outside of yes, or no at the altar, means not worthy; however, whoever says yes, or no and leaves Love (gift) upon the altar; you said he is guilty?

KJV Matthew 23: verse 19

Ye fools and blind: for whether *is* greater, the gift, or the altar that sanctifieth the gift?

Comment appropriately to "*Ye* fools and blind: for whether *is* greater, the gift, or the altar that sanctifieth the gift?"

Once again, you deceivers and con artists: therefore, what is uttermost, the Love (gift), or the house of worship (alter) that declares the Love unrighteous.

KJV Matthew 23: verse 20

Whoso therefore shall swear by the altar, sweareth by it, and by all things thereon.

Comment appropriately to "Whoso therefore shall swear by the altar, sweareth by it, and by all things thereon."

Therefore, whosoever shall make promises falsely (swear by the altar), lives with strong disapproval in the subconscious mind and by all thoughts is consciously aware (thereon).

KJV Matthew 23: verse 21

And whoso shall swear by the temple, sweareth by it, and by

him that dwelleth therein.

Comment appropriately to "And whoso shall swear by the temple, sweareth by it, and by him that dwelleth therein."

Also, whoever shall make promises (swear) outside of yes, or no of themselves (the temple), again, lives with a disapproval within the subconscious evilness dwells therein.

KJV Matthew 23: verse 22

And he that shall swear by heaven, sweareth by the throne of God, and by him that sitteth thereon.

Comment appropriately to "And he that shall swear by heaven, sweareth by the throne of God, and by him that sitteth thereon."

Accordingly, he affirms that the consciousness of thought will indeed reap wrongdoings of the idea before God, likewise, to our Lord, which sits next to the Father.

KJV Matthew 23: verse 23

Woe unto you, scribes and Pharisees, hypocrites! for ye pay tithe of mint and anise and cummin, and have omitted the weightier *matters* of the law, judgment, mercy, and faith: these ought ye to have done, and not to leave the other undone.

Comment appropriately to "Woe unto you, scribes and Pharisees, hypocrites! for ye pay tithe of mint and anise and cummin,"

With this purpose, suffering unto you holy men of God, you con artist! How dare you make your churchgoers receive disturbed knowledge (mint), unworthy truths (anise), and damaging emotional memorization (cumin) in mind.

Note: At any rate, tithing was a form of exchange regardless of its condition or materials.

Comment appropriately to "and have omitted the weightier *matters* of the law, judgment, mercy, and faith: these ought ye to have done, and not to leave the other undone."

However, you have foregone governing matters such as regulations, perception, forgiveness, and belief, for, in principle, men of the cloth should address these matters instead of the others concerning the tithe.

KJV Matthew 23: verse 24

Ye blind guides, which strain at a gnat, and swallow a camel.

Comment appropriately to "*Ye* blind guides, which strain at a gnat, and swallow a camel."

Oh, your spiritual blind guides of the Old Testament. You stress (strain) and worry over a flea, all the while a critical elephant walks through your house.

KJV Matthew 23: verse 25

Woe unto you, scribes and Pharisees, hypocrites! for ye make clean the outside of the cup and of the platter, but within they are full of extortion and excess.

Comment appropriately to "Woe unto you, scribes and Pharisees, hypocrites! for ye make clean the outside of the cup and of the platter, but within they are full of extortion and excess."

Accordingly, misery unto the men of the cloth, you tricksters! Indeed, you do not take matters of the heart (cup) and your inner speech (platter), all the while you are full of anger (extortion) and greed (excess).

KJV Matthew 23: verse 26

Thou blind Pharisee, cleanse first that *which is* within the cup and platter, that the outside of them may be clean also.

Comment appropriately to "*Thou* blind Pharisee, cleanse first that *which is* within the cup and platter, that the outside of them may be clean also."

Consequently, spiritually blind holy men, take matters of the heart with Love (cup) first. Afterward, take on righteous thinking, in mind clearing your speech (platter). Then, you will see the true outer self-being sound mind and body.

KJV Matthew 23: verse 27

Woe unto you, scribes and Pharisees, hypocrites! for ye are like unto whited sepulchres, which indeed appear beautiful outward, but are within full of dead *men's* bones, and of all uncleanness.

Comment appropriately to "Woe unto you, scribes and Pharisees, hypocrites! for ye are like unto whited sepulchres, which indeed appear beautiful outward, but are within full of dead *men's* bones, and of all uncleanness."

Furthermore, sorrow unto you, deceitful holy men, phony impostors! Again, you are such purity-looking bleached on the outside full of light. However, inwardly, you are unclean, dead spiritually, and most unrighteous.

KJV Matthew 23: verse 28

Even so ye also outwardly appear righteous unto men, but within ye are full of hypocrisy and iniquity.

Comment appropriately to "Even so ye also outwardly appear righteous unto men, but within ye are full of hypocrisy and iniquity."

As a result, you seem presentable outwardly as a righteous saint; however, inwardly, you are filled with inner anger of unfair logic as a wolf in sheep's clothing.

KJV Matthew 23: verse 29

Woe unto you, scribes and Pharisees, hypocrites! because ye build the tombs of the prophets, and garnish the sepulchres of the righteous,

Comment appropriately to "Woe unto you, scribes and Pharisees, hypocrites! because ye build the tombs of the prophets, and garnish the sepulchres of the righteous,"

To this end, misery unto you, a men of the cloth, (scribes and Pharisees) you crook! Although you build tombstones for the leaders of your synagogue; thus, decorating them as if they were saints before the church.

KJV Matthew 23: verse 30

And say, If we had been in the days of our fathers, we would not have been partakers with them in the blood of the prophets.

Comment appropriately to "And say, If we had been in the days of our fathers, we would not have been partakers with them in the blood of the prophets."

Thus, you say, if we had lived back in the old time with our mentors. Indeed, we wouldn't have been so evil or laid our hands on those prophesiers.

KJV Matthew 23: verse 31

Wherefore ye be witnesses unto yourselves, that ye are the children of them which killed the prophets.

Comment appropriately to "Wherefore ye be witnesses unto yourselves, that ye are the children of them which killed the prophets."

Hence, for a reason, you shall become witnesses to demise as though you sought out the same ending. For you are the children of your ancestors and with the same demeanor.

KJV Matthew 23: verse 32

Fill ye up then the measure of your fathers.

Comment appropriately to "Fill ye up then the measure of your fathers."

Unfortunately, your sins are in alignment (measure) with your ancestors.

KJV Matthew 23: verse 33

Ye serpents, *ye* generation of vipers, how can ye escape the damnation of hell?

Comment appropriately to "*Ye* serpents, *ye* generation of vipers, how can ye escape the damnation of hell?"

Consequently, you are with unrighteous desires (serpents) and temptations (vipers); how long shall you remain in your divided mind (damnation of hell) of your alter ego.

KJV Matthew 23: verse 34

Wherefore, behold, I send unto you prophets, and wise men, and scribes: and *some* of them ye shall kill and crucify; and *some* of them shall ye scourge in your synagogues, and persecute *them* from city to city:

Comment appropriately to "Wherefore, behold, I send unto you prophets, and wise men, and scribes: and *some* of them ye shall kill and crucify; and *some* of them shall ye scourge in your synagogues, and persecute *them* from city to city:"

Therefore, observe others as prophets, knowledgeable men, transcribers, and thus, you have murdered them in the subconscious mind. Also, some prophets will become devoured in mind.

As a result, some will suffer severe torture in consciousness.

KJV Matthew 23: verse 35

That upon you may come all the righteous blood shed upon the earth, from the blood of righteous Abel unto the blood of Zacharias son of Barachias, whom ye slew between the temple and the altar.

Comment appropriately to "That upon you may come all the righteous blood shed upon the earth, from the blood of righteous Abel unto the blood of Zacharias son of Barachias, whom ye slew between the temple and the altar."

Therefore, upon completion of righteous thinking of a spiritual awakening, the resurrection of the enlightened being shall endure in a like manner as Abel and Zacharias, son of Brachial.

Yet, they were consciously tortured in mind and at the tabernacle.

KJV Matthew 23: verse 36

Verily I say unto you, All these things shall come upon this generation.

Comment appropriately to "Verily I say unto you,"

Be wise and alert to truths for entering the kingdom of heaven.

Comment appropriately to "All these things shall come upon this generation."

Indeed, all things before prophesied shall be unto this society.

KJV Matthew 23: verse 37

O Jerusalem, Jerusalem, *thou* that killest the prophets, and stonest them which are sent unto thee, how often would I have gathered thy children together, even as a hen gathereth her chickens under *her* wings, and ye would not!

Comment appropriately to "O Jerusalem, Jerusalem, *thou* that killest the prophets, and stonest them which are sent unto thee, how often would I have gathered thy children together, even as a hen gathereth her chickens under *her* wings, and ye would not!"

Indeed, the Kingdom of Heaven, for many prophecies have you persecuted in mind offering a barrage of insults (stoning). Therefore, oh Lord, be a protective shield in thy sight, and for how long shall we stand in wait.

Hence, the Lord shall come to gather his sheep amongst the wolves and protect his flock with his rod!

KJV Matthew 23: verse 38

Behold, your house is left unto you desolate.

Comment appropriately to "Behold, your house is left unto you desolate."

To this end, your soul (house) is left torn and tired.

KJV Matthew 23: verse 39

For I say unto you, Ye shall not see me henceforth, till ye shall say, Blessed *is* he that cometh in the name of the Lord.

Comment appropriately to "For I say unto you, Ye shall not see me henceforth, till ye shall say, Blessed *is* he that cometh in the name of the Lord."

For these are my New Commandments, until you have done the works given unto you will not see me; until that such moment, you shall say, blessed are those that our Lord cometh unto them on high.

Matthew Chapter 24

KJV Matthew 24: verse 2

And Jesus said unto them, See ye not all these things? verily I say unto you, There shall not be left here one stone upon another, that shall not be thrown down.

Comment appropriately to "See ye not all these things? verily I say unto you,"

See what is before you because I tell you that I have come to fulfill the assignment that my Father has given unto me, the Messiah.

Comment appropriately to "There shall not be left here one stone upon another, that shall not be thrown down."

Therefore, I lay my life down (stone upon another) for all to see my works. It is by my will (not be thrown down) and a willingness to bring it back in the consciousness of the Father.

KJV Matthew 24: verse 4

And Jesus answered and said unto them, Take heed that no

man deceive you.

Comment appropriately to "Take heed that no man deceive you."

Therefore, believe upon the words of Jesus Christ and lean not unto men and their evil mind.

KJV Matthew 24: verse 5

For many shall come in my name, saying, I am Christ; and shall deceive many.

Comment appropriately to "For many shall come in my name, saying, I am Christ; and shall deceive many."

Be wiser than those with evil intent, for many will use my name in vain, saying "In Jesus Christ Name." For this reason, they will not have sincerity in their heart.

KJV Matthew 24: verse 6

And ye shall hear of wars and rumours of wars: see that ye be not troubled: for all *these things* must come to pass, but the end is not yet.

Comment appropriately to "And ye shall hear of wars and rumours of wars: see that ye be not troubled: for all *these things* must come to pass, but the end is not yet."

Therefore, be not troubled in your heart because of evil men presenting bloodshed and rumors of conflict.

Rest in my peace: for these events must come to be in lessons of Love which leads to my second coming.

KJV Matthew 24: verse 7

For nation shall rise against nation, and kingdom against kingdom: and there shall be famines, and pestilences, and earthquakes, in divers places.

Comment appropriately to "For nation shall rise against nation, and kingdom against kingdom: and there shall be famines, and pestilences, and earthquakes, in divers places."

Consequently, there shall be alter ego (nation) versus alter ego (human mind) of wrongful evildoers against one another for earthly power.

More importantly, emotional conflict of power and earthly riches (kingdom against kingdom) will arise.

For this reason, Love and truth will remain scarce and deficient (famines) while unbalancing subconscious emotions produce disease (pestilences) within because of their unrighteous desires.

Although underlying truths are hidden below lies in the mind (earthquakes), they are indeed beneath emotions in the subconscious mind (waters of diverse places).

KJV Matthew 24: verse 8

All these *are* the beginning of sorrows.

Comment appropriately to "All these *are* the beginning of sorrows."

Indeed, unintended thoughts which lead to the heart are the

beginning of agony and repentance.

KJV Matthew 24: verse 9

Then shall they deliver you up to be afflicted, and shall kill you: and ye shall be hated of all nations for my name's sake.

Comment appropriately to "Then shall they deliver you up to be afflicted, and shall kill you: and ye shall be hated of all nations for my name's sake."

For this reason, men shall revile (affliction) against you in their alter ego (human mind); therefore, evil anger (kill) from within because of your righteousness for Jesus' name's sake.

KJV Matthew 24: verse 10

And then shall many be offended, and shall betray one another, and shall hate one another.

Comment appropriately to "And then shall many be offended, and shall betray one another, and shall hate one another."

Truthfully, inwardly they will repent to what is true (offended), and they shall betray truth versus evil in the subconscious mind.

Therefore, because of this, there will be inner hatred of lies from the human mind.

KJV Matthew 24: verse 11

And many false prophets shall rise, and shall deceive many.

Comment appropriately to "And many false prophets shall rise, and shall deceive many."

More importantly, deceivers and men of great lies arise and will mislead hundreds of thousands.

KJV Matthew 24: verse 12

And because iniquity shall abound, the love of many shall wax cold.

Comment appropriately to "And because iniquity shall abound, the love of many shall wax cold."

Evidently, in all unfairness in deceiving many, the feelings of Love shall not be felt upon many, for they will feel lost (wax cold) in the world.

KJV Matthew 24: verse 13

But he that shall endure unto the end, the same shall be saved.

Comment appropriately to "But he that shall endure unto the end, the same shall be saved."

Equally important, for whoever shall find peace (endure) in the subconscious mind shall remain until everlasting and find Love and truth.

KJV Matthew 24: verse 14

And this gospel of the kingdom shall be preached in all the world for a witness unto all nations; and then shall the end come.

Comment appropriately to "And this gospel of the kingdom shall be preached in all the world for a witness unto all nations; and then shall the end come."

Furthermore, the great news (gospels) of our Lord and Savior shall reach each end of the earth in consciousness. Love and truth shall receive many facts to all (nations) in consciousness (ending come).

KJV Matthew 24: verse 15

When ye therefore shall see the abomination of desolation, spoken of by Daniel the prophet, stand in the holy place, (whoso readeth, let him understand:)

Comment appropriately to "When ye therefore shall see the abomination of desolation, spoken of by Daniel the prophet, stand in the holy place, (whoso readeth, let him understand:)."

In other words, when you see tremendous anger (abomination of desolation) and hatred in the media, these events were foretold by the prophet Daniel in the old time.

Furthermore, a society of destruction against one another for their lack of Love and truth shall end in darkness unless forgiveness becomes conscious thinking.

Understand, Jesus is near awaiting your commitment to honor the kingdom of heaven.

KJV Matthew 24: verse 16

Then let them which be in Judaea flee into the mountains:

Comment appropriately to "Then let them which be in Judaea flee into the mountains:"

Additionally, let those who understand the inner workings (Judaea) of the heart and mind surrender to the Father's consciousness (mountains).

KJV Matthew 24: verse 17

Let him which is on the housetop not come down to take any thing out of his house:

Comment appropriately to "Let him which is on the housetop not come down to take any thing out of his house:"

Moreover, allow those able to accept truths in consciousness to avoid withholding Love within the soul (house).

KJV Matthew 24: verse 18

Neither let him which is in the field return back to take his clothes.

Comment appropriately to "Neither let him which is in the field return back to take his clothes."

In like manner, do not allow those with an understanding of conscious thought in the subconscious mind to return to the physical sense (clothing) of the altered ego.

KJV Matthew 24: verse 19

And woe unto them that are with child, and to them that give suck in those days!

Comment appropriately to "And woe unto them that are with child, and to them that give suck in those days!"

Equally important, dismiss troubles of those who desire (a child) to enter the kingdom of heaven nonetheless, those who truly gave birth in the mind of those desires.

KJV Matthew 24: verse 20

But pray ye that your flight be not in the winter, neither on the sabbath day:

Comment appropriately to "But pray ye that your flight be not in the winter, neither on the sabbath day:"

Therefore, give thanks that your desires to enter the kingdom of heaven are not in darkness (winter) nor in the time of rest (sabbath).

KJV Matthew 24: verse 21

For then shall be great tribulation, such as was not since the beginning of the world to this time, no, nor ever shall be.

Comment appropriately to "For then shall be great tribulation, such as was not since the beginning of the world to this time, no, nor ever shall be."

As a result, there will be enormous disturbances in the subconscious mind from all the evilness.

But conversely, there will be times where evil will prevail as in the beginning; thus, along with times where there is little rest for the mind.

KJV Matthew 24: verse 22

And except those days should be shortened, there should no flesh be saved: but for the elect's sake those days shall be shortened.

Comment appropriately to "And except those days should be shortened, there should no flesh be saved: but for the elect's sake those days shall be shortened."

Additionally, there will be days when it feels lesser in awareness, for there will be no spiritual life (no flesh) to handle a higher vibration because the disciple (Chosen elect) must realign within the mind.

KJV Matthew 24: verse 23

Then if any man shall say unto you, Lo, here *is* Christ, or there; believe *it* not.

Comment appropriately to "Then if any man shall say unto you, Lo, here *is* Christ, or there; believe *it* not."

Therefore, if men shall deceive you in consciousness, thereby saying Yeah, in my ministry (Lo), you'll find God's Kingdom. So again, could you not believe it?

KJV Matthew 24: verse 24

For there shall arise false Christs, and false prophets, and shall shew great signs and wonders; insomuch that, if *it were* possible, they shall deceive the very elect.

Comment appropriately to "For there shall arise false

Christs, and false prophets, and shall shew great signs and wonders; insomuch that, if *it were* possible, they shall deceive the very elect."

Consequently, assemble of the deceitful televangelist (false prophets) who testifies on untruths luring falsehood of miracle (signs and wonders) while in the presence of many.

Notwithstanding, followers (elects) looking for guidance are misled and deceived until truths harden their hearts.

KJV Matthew 24: verse 25

Behold, I have told you before.

Comment appropriately to "Behold, I have told you before."

For sure, Christ has warned you from creation.

KJV Matthew 24: verse 26

Wherefore if they shall say unto you, Behold, he is in the desert; go not forth: behold, *he* is in the secret chambers; believe *it* not.

Comment appropriately to "Wherefore if they shall say unto you, Behold, he is in the desert; go not forth: behold, *he* is in the secret chambers; believe *it* not."

For this purpose, when they tell you, seek heaven in the divided devilish mind, do not believe them. For Christ resides in the subconscious truths and not the lies beneath the oceans of emotions.

Thus, if they tell you, seek heaven in a chamber unseen by Christ, do not allow these deceitful intentions to manifest. For these chambers are in the consciousness of heaven where our Father dwells and sees all things.

KJV Matthew 24: verse 27

For as the lightning cometh out of the east, and shineth even unto the west; so shall also the coming of the Son of man be.

Comment appropriately to "For as the lightning cometh out of the east, and shineth even unto the west; so shall also the coming of the Son of man be."

With this purpose in mind, on your journey to enlightenment by day (east), the warmth of understanding fills the light.

Nonetheless, by the evening of sunset (west) of a soul's cycle of desires - hence, the second coming in his Glory Jesus will be.

KJV Matthew 24: verse 28

For wheresoever the carcase is, there will the eagles be gathered together.

Comment appropriately to "For wheresoever the carcase is, there will the eagles be gathered together."

Therefore, whoever is spiritually dead (carcass) in mind, there you'll find thoughts of confusion (eagles) gathered in the subconscious mind.

KJV Matthew 24: verse 29

Immediately after the tribulation of those days shall the sun be darkened, and the moon shall not give her light, and the stars shall fall from heaven, and the powers of the heavens shall be shaken:

Comment appropriately to "Immediately after the tribulation of those days shall the sun be darkened, and the moon shall not give her light:"

As a result, the torment in the subconscious mind in the light (day) of warmth quickly merged into the evening darkness. When the heat has no light (moon) upon itself, swiftly it takes no warming, and the shadow of emptiness falls on the soul.

Comment appropriately to "and the stars shall fall from heaven, and the powers of the heavens shall be shaken."

Accordingly, the evening falls upon complete darkness in the light flicker (star fall) from consciousness; thus, the impression of awareness is lost (shaken).

KJV Matthew 24: verse 30

And then shall appear the sign of the Son of man in heaven: and then shall all the tribes of the earth mourn, and they shall see the Son of man coming in the clouds of heaven with power and great glory.

Comment appropriately to "And then shall appear the sign of the Son of man in heaven: and then shall all the tribes of the earth mourn,"

Indeed, in full consciousness of the Holy Spirit, all the subconscious awakening of the divided mind shall not live (mourn) anymore.

Comment appropriately to "and they shall see the Son of man coming in the clouds of heaven with power and great glory."

Equally important, every soul shall see our Lord's dominance and triumph in the consciousness of our Heavenly Father.

KJV Matthew 24: verse 31

And he shall send his angels with a great sound of a trumpet, and they shall gather together his elect from the four winds, from one end of heaven to the other.

Comment appropriately to "And he shall send his angels with a great sound of a trumpet, and they shall gather together his elect from the four winds, from one end of heaven to the other."

Thus, the Lord thy God shall send a multitude of energies (angels) rejoicing upon the disciple (Chosen elect) who has obtained deep consciousness of the Self (four winds).

Alas, in all parts of the mind (conscious, subconscious, and heart) and the soul's nature (heaven).

KJV Matthew 24: verse 32

Now learn a parable of the fig tree; When his branch is yet tender, and putteth forth leaves, ye know that summer *is* nigh:

Comment appropriately to "Now learn a parable of the fig tree; When his branch is yet tender, and putteth forth leaves, ye know that summer *is* nigh:"

Accordingly, I become aware (learn) of how to remain in my peace (parables). Finally, when the chosen elect is mindful of conscious thoughts that lead to unconditional Love (tender).

He places the wrongdoings of others instantly to forgiveness as compassion offers passive guidance (forth leaves) to all.

For this reason, the disciple of Christ's light shines within the cycle (summer) of a soul's desire for completion to enlightenment.

KJV Matthew 24: verse 33

So likewise ye, when ye shall see all these things, know that it is near, *even* at the doors.

Comment appropriately to "So likewise ye, when ye shall see all these things, know that it is near, *even* at the doors."

Become aware when you see these things manifesting in your wholeness. Be mindful; completion is near (at the door).

KJV Matthew 24: verse 34

Verily I say unto you, This generation shall not pass, till all these things be fulfilled.

Comment appropriately to "Verily I say unto you, This generation shall not pass, till all these things be fulfilled."

Listen upon these truths for entering the kingdom of God; this society will not enter the kingdom until it has completed the works given to it by the Father.

KJV Matthew 24: verse 35

Heaven and earth shall pass away, but my words shall not pass away.

Comment appropriately to "Heaven and earth shall pass away, but my words shall not pass away."

This physical body (heaven and earth) shall yet pass away in the material world in all righteousness. By thy glory of the New Testament, God's word shall never pass away!

KJV Matthew 24: verse 36

But of that day and hour knoweth no *man*, no, not the angels of heaven, but my Father only.

Comment appropriately to "But of that day and hour knoweth no *man*, no, not the angels of heaven, but my Father only."

In this gladness, in completing enlightenment in a soul's cycle (day or hour), no physical human being (no man) can know.

The truth of giving the Kingdom of God comes by way of the Father; through his Love, children of God shall fulfill ye.

KJV Matthew 24: verse 37

But as the days of Noe *were*, so shall also the coming of the Son of man be.

Comment appropriately to "But as the days of Noe *were*, so shall also the coming of the Son of man be."

Therefore, as with Noah (Noe) in the book of old with floods, the rise of consciousness shall come like the Son of man will be.

KJV Matthew 24: verse 38

For as in the days that were before the flood they were eating and drinking, marrying and giving in marriage, until the day that Noe entered into the ark,

Comment appropriately to "For as in the days that were before the flood they were eating and drinking, marrying and giving in marriage, until the day that Noe entered into the ark,"

At that time and even before the floods, many neglected works were given unto them by the Father. Thus, doing as they please without spiritual obtainment. (Eating, drinking, festivities).

Well, at least until the ark doors of Noah were shut.

KJV Matthew 24: verse 39

And knew not until the flood came, and took them all away; so shall also the coming of the Son of man be.

Comment appropriately to "And knew not until the flood came, and took them all away; so shall also the coming of the Son of man be."

For this reason, they did not seek truths of the kingdom and when the floods were upon them! Their repentance was unable to be received because the end had come.

Thus, on the last day, when we stand to give an account of our life, so shall it be before God.

KJV Matthew 24: verse 40

Then shall two be in the field; the one shall be taken, and the other left.

Comment appropriately to "Then shall two be in the field; the one shall be taken, and the other left."

Hence, before God in consciousness shall we stand, the Lord shall take the mind of the human body away (one shall be taken). Therefore, we remain in God's Love in the oneness of the Father.

KJV Matthew 24: verse 41

Two *women shall* be grinding at the mill; the one shall be taken, and the other left.

Comment appropriately to "Two *women shall* be grinding at the mill; the one shall be taken, and the other left."

Furthermore, thy Lord shall take the human consciousness of the Self away to leave truth in place (two women) during the journey upon the face of the early plain.

Note: The mind of the soul is the female. The soul is male.

KJV Matthew 24: verse 42

Watch therefore: for ye know not what hour your Lord doth come.

Comment appropriately to "Watch therefore: for ye know not what hour your Lord doth come."

For this reason, do the works the Father has given to you. As a result, you do not know when the hour of our Lord receives (doth) you in paradise.

KJV Matthew 24: verse 43

But know this, that if the goodman of the house had known in what watch the thief would come, he would have watched, and would not have suffered his house to be broken up.

Comment appropriately to "But know this, that if the goodman of the house had known in what watch the thief would come, he would have watched,"

Therefore, if the Lord (goodman) had informed the soul (house) and known the end was to come, he would have done the work given to it by the Father.

Comment appropriately to "and would not have suffered his house to be broken up."

Otherwise, he would have been able to protect his conscious

way of thinking from the Father. However, It was allowed to be misguided by men (thieves) and the things of this world.

KJV Matthew 24: verse 44

Therefore be ye also ready: for in such an hour as ye think not the Son of man cometh.

Comment appropriately to "Therefore be ye also ready: for in such an hour as ye think not the Son of man cometh."

For this reason, be ready when the time comes near for the end. Consequently, you do not know when thy Lord shall come to you in the future.

KJV Matthew 24: verse 45

Who then is a faithful and wise servant, whom his lord hath made ruler over his household, to give them meat in due season?

Comment appropriately to "Who then is a faithful and wise servant, whom his lord hath made ruler over his household, to give them meat in due season?"

Therefore, who has genuinely accepted my New Commandment and taken them into their heart (faithful and wise servants).

Thus, thy Lord has made the ruler over your soul with free will and will give you spiritual truths upon your journey.

KJV Matthew 24: verse 46

Blessed *is* that servant, whom his lord when he cometh shall find so doing.

Comment appropriately to "Blessed *is* that servant, whom his lord when he cometh shall find so doing."

Indeed, blessed is he that doeth the work of the Father when thy Lord shall find him in spirit.

KJV Matthew 24: verse 47

Verily I say unto you, That he shall make him ruler over all his goods.

Comment appropriately to "Verily I say unto you, That he shall make him ruler over all his goods."

Learn these things in my New Commandments; only you can do these works within Self with your Lord to full consciousness.

KJV Matthew 24: verse 48

But and if that evil servant shall say in his heart, My lord delayeth his coming;

Comment appropriately to "But and if that evil servant shall say in his heart, My lord delayeth his coming;."

However, if thyself (the evil servant) says within the consciousness of the heart, where is my Lord for he isn't here or doesn't show himself to me.

KJV Matthew 24: verse 49

And shall begin to smite *his* fellowservants, and to eat and drink with the drunken;

Comment appropriately to "And shall begin to smite *his* fellowservants, and to eat and drink with the drunken;."

Therefore, he becomes aggressive (smite) to his brothers and sisters (fellow servants) while persecuting (drunken) them verbally and in mind.

KJV Matthew 24: verse 50

The lord of that servant shall come in a day when he looketh not for *him*, and in an hour that he is not aware of,

Comment appropriately to "The lord of that servant shall come in a day when he looketh not for *him*, and in an hour that he is not aware of."

Indeed, thy Lord God shall come unto him that portrays evildoings unto others in a time when he is not aware of his presence.

KJV Matthew 24: verse 51

And shall cut him asunder, and appoint *him* his portion with the hypocrites: there shall be weeping and gnashing of teeth.

Comment appropriately to "And shall cut him asunder, and appoint *him* his portion with the hypocrites: there shall be weeping and gnashing of teeth."

Consequently, thy Lord shall indeed cast his wrongdoings

out of his consciousness and give their account of treatment to return for the sake of Love and truth. You have been misled on your journey and because of your misdeeds.

In truth, the soul will realize true repentance and deep sorrow (weeping and gnashing of teeth).

Matthew Chapter 25

KJV Matthew 25: verse 1

Then shall the kingdom of heaven be likened unto ten virgins, which took their lamps, and went forth to meet the bridegroom.

Comment appropriately to "Then shall the kingdom of heaven be likened unto ten virgins, which took their lamps, and went forth to meet the bridegroom."

Indeed, this is for your awareness of things concerning the kingdom of heaven. For this reason, the domain is likened to a mind unaware and in search of knowledge and understanding.

Thus, it hasn't any awareness of its true nature outside of the kingdom upon taking its light (lamp) to a foreign land (earth or other places outside of the domain).

In addition, it went out in search of its true nature in the efforts of enlightenment (meet the bridegroom).

KJV Matthew 25: verse 2

And five of them were wise, and five *were* foolish.

Comment appropriately to "And five of them were wise, and five *were* foolish."

Nonetheless, five of the virgin minds prepared well before they departed from the kingdom of heaven.

KJV Matthew 25: verse 3

They that *were* foolish took their lamps, and took no oil with them:

Comment appropriately to "They that *were* foolish took their lamps, and took no oil with them:"

Even more so, the five virgin minds took no awareness (oil) into their purpose upon searching for the bridegroom.

KJV Matthew 25: verse 4

But the wise took oil in their vessels with their lamps.

Comment appropriately to "But the wise took oil in their vessels with their lamps."

Notwithstanding, the wise souls took awareness (oil) in their conscious light to seek the righteousness of the bridegroom.

KJV Matthew 25: verse 5

While the bridegroom tarried, they all slumbered and slept.

Comment appropriately to "While the bridegroom tarried,

they all slumbered and slept."

Once more, while the Lord wasn't entirely in their awareness, most felt weary of separation (slumbered) because of darkness (slept).

KJV Matthew 25: verse 6

And at midnight there was a cry made, Behold, the bridegroom cometh; go ye out to meet him.

Comment appropriately to "And at midnight there was a cry made, Behold, the bridegroom cometh; go ye out to meet him."

So, when the time (midnight) came, a sound of sorrow (cry) was clear indeed; the Lord was near. Thus, the virgin mind made itself ready to receive his arrival.

Note: In this parable, midnight refers to a part of a soul's cycle when **NO spiritual work** can be done to reach enlightenment. In this case, the soul is in the darkness of the light within itself.

KJV Matthew 25: verse 7

Then all those virgins arose, and trimmed their lamps.

Comment appropriately to "Then all those virgins arose and trimmed their lamps."

Likewise, with the arrival of the Lord, the mind made itself aware of the higher Self in its vibrational alignment (virgin arose) to allow its light (lamp) for greater clarity.

KJV Matthew 25: verse 8

And the foolish said unto the wise, Give us of your oil; for our lamps are gone out.

Comment appropriately to "And the foolish said unto the wise, Give us of your oil; for our lamps are gone out."

Furthermore, the lower vibrational mind (foolish) says to the higher vibrational reason (wise). Please share your awareness (oil) with us so that we, too, will see the light of understanding clearly as you do.

Notwithstanding, it could not be because the virgin mind, without awareness (oil) of its vibration of wisdom and light, was low (gone out).

KJV Matthew 25: verse 9

But the wise answered, saying, *Not so*; lest there be not enough for us and you: but go ye rather to them that sell, and buy for yourselves.

Comment appropriately to "But the wise answered, saying, *Not so*; lest there be not enough for us and you:"

Nonetheless, the higher vibration (wise) said to the lower vibration virgin mind, no, we cannot allow for our awareness (oil) to enter your lamps. What we have is an abundance for us to use inside of our domain.

Comment appropriately to "but go ye rather to them that sell, and buy for yourselves."

However, sell all that you have to the poor (empty all worldly goods) and store up what is spiritual for the kingdom for yourselves.

KJV Matthew 25: verse 10

And while they went to buy, the bridegroom came; and they that were ready went in with him to the marriage: and the door was shut.

Comment appropriately to "And while they went to buy, the bridegroom came; and they that were ready went in with him to the marriage: and the door was shut."

Accordingly, when they gave up all their worldly goods (went to buy oil), the Lord came in the night. The wise with awareness (oil) was ready to receive the bridegroom (marriage) with joy and evolve into enlightenment (door was shut).

KJV Matthew 25: verse 11

Afterward came also the other virgins, saying, Lord, Lord, open to us.

Comment appropriately to "Afterward came also the other virgins, saying, Lord, Lord, open to us."

Nonetheless, the other lesser vibrational souls who went out to give to the poor came back to cry out, Lord God, the Good Shepherd. Please, allow us to enter the kingdom!

KJV Mathew 25: verse 12

But he answered and said, Verily I say unto you, I know you

not.

Comment appropriately to "But he answered and said, Verily I say unto you, I know you not."

Therefore, I tell you these truths for entering the kingdom of heaven, for if you do not do the works given to you by the Father. Indeed, I will not come to know you in the kingdom of heaven.

KJV Matthew 25: verse 13

Watch therefore, for ye know neither the day nor the hour wherein the Son of man cometh.

Comment appropriately to "Watch therefore, for ye know neither the day nor the hour wherein the Son of man cometh."

For this reason, become aware of your gladness because you do not know when thy Lord God is seeking you in the truth of the kingdom. Therefore, do the works given unto you by the Father in heaven.

KJV Matthew 25: verse 14

For *the kingdom of heaven is* as a man travelling into a far country, *who* called his own servants, and delivered unto them his goods.

Comment appropriately to "For *the kingdom of heaven is* as a man travelling into a far country, *who* called his own servants, and delivered unto them his goods."

Likewise, the kingdom of heaven is like a man traveling to

another country.

However, he develops an awareness of spiritual angels (servants) on his journey and allows them access to his spiritual needs (goods).

KJV Matthew 25: verse 15

And unto one he gave five talents, to another two, and to another one; to every man according to his several ability; and straightway took his journey.

Comment appropriately to "And unto one he gave five talents, to another two, and to another one; to every man according to his several ability; and straightway took his journey."

Thus, the Father gave each man according to his works. Therefore, he gave one soul five hundred times his value of awareness in the kingdom, another three hundred times his value, and yet, another one hundred times his value.

Upon receiving their assignment, they immediately (straightway) continued their journey to incarnate (took a physical body).

KJV Matthew 25: verse 16

Then he that had received the five talents went and traded with the same, and made *them* other five talents.

Comment appropriately to "Then he that had received the five talents went and traded with the same, and made *them* other five talents."

Likewise, the soul which had five times his value in the kingdom more than doubled his value of awareness in consciousness from five to ten times.

KJV Matthew 25: verse 17

And likewise he that *had received* two, he also gained other two.

Comment appropriately to "And likewise he that *had received* two, he also gained other two."

In addition, the soul which had two times his value of Love in the kingdom more than doubled his value from two to four times.

KJV Matthew 25: verse 18

But he that had received one went and digged in the earth, and hid his lord's money.

Comment appropriately to "But he that had received one went and digged in the earth, and hid his lord's money."

However, one soul took his Lord's wealth and hid it within the subconscious mind (earth of the alter-ego mind).

KJV Matthew 25: verse 19

After a long time the lord of those servants cometh, and reckoneth with them.

Comment appropriately to "After a long time the lord of those servants cometh, and reckoneth with them."

Even more so, after time had elapsed and momentarily from the awareness of his Lord.

In so much as each soul returned home to exchange what additional wealth they had obtained on its journey.

KJV Matthew 25: verse 20

And so he that had received five talents came and brought other five talents, saying, Lord, thou deliveredst unto me five talents: behold, I have gained beside them five talents more.

Comment appropriately to "And so he that had received five talents came and brought other five talents, saying, Lord, thou deliveredst unto me five talents: behold, I have gained beside them five talents more."

In essence, he returns to his Lord and states, see my Lord God; I have returned with more than double of my goods than I received.

Indeed, you gave me five, and I returned with ten times more their value of happiness, joy, and abundant prosperity in the heart, soul, and mind.

KJV Matthew 25: verse 21

His lord said unto him, Well done, *thou* good and faithful servant: thou hast been faithful over a few things, I will make thee ruler over many things: enter thou into the joy of thy lord.

Comment appropriately to "His lord said unto him, Well done, *thou* good and faithful servant: thou hast been faithful over a few things, I will make thee ruler over many things: enter thou into the joy of thy lord."

Thus, saith the Lord, phenomenal job, my faithful servant seeking righteousness in the heart, soul, and mind (few things). In due season, I will make pure in all things concerning consciousness.

Enter my kingdom with gladness in the Father.

KJV Matthew 25: verse 22

He also that had received two talents came and said, Lord, thou deliveredst unto me two talents: behold, I have gained two other talents beside them.

Comment appropriately to "He also that had received two talents came and said, Lord, thou deliveredst unto me two talents: behold, I have gained two other talents beside them."

Likewise, he also returned to his Lord and said, see my Lord God; I also returned with more than double my two goods than I received.

Even more so, you gave me two, and I returned with four times more their value of happiness, joy, and abundant prosperity in the heart, soul, and mind.

KJV Matthew 25: verse 23

His lord said unto him, Well done, good and faithful servant; thou hast been faithful over a few things, I will make thee ruler over many things: enter thou into the joy of thy lord.

Comment appropriately to "His lord said unto him, Well done, good and faithful servant; thou hast been faithful over a few things, I will make thee ruler over many things: enter thou into the joy of thy lord."

Once again, the Lord said to his next servant. You have done a superb job, my faithful servant seeking righteousness in the heart, soul, and mind (few things). In due season, I will make pure in all things concerning consciousness.

Enter my kingdom with gladness in the Father.

KJV Matthew 25: verse 24

Then he which had received the one talent came and said, Lord, I knew thee that thou art an hard man, reaping where thou hast not sown, and gathering where thou hast not strawed:

Comment appropriately to "Then he which had received the one talent came and said, Lord, I knew thee that thou art an hard man, reaping where thou hast not sown, and gathering where thou hast not strawed:"

Afterward, the soul that received one passion returned to his Lord at the end of days.

Thus, saying Lord, indeed, you are the creator of all things, for thy kingdom comes of all Love and truths (reaping where thou hast not sown), and receiving eternal devotion ceaselessly.

KJV Matthew 25: verse 25

And I was afraid, and went and hid thy talent in the earth: lo, *there* thou hast *that* is thine.

Comment appropriately to "And I was afraid, and went and hid thy talent in the earth: lo, *there* thou hast *that* is thine."

Furthermore, I did not desire to lose any passion stored within me on my journey, hiding it deep within my subconscious mind. This way, I returned without losing that thy Lord had trusted me with my consciousness.

KJV Matthew 25: verse 26

His lord answered and said unto him, *Thou* wicked and slothful servant, thou knewest that I reap where I sowed not, and gather where I have not strawed:

Comment appropriately to "His lord answered and said unto him, *Thou* wicked and slothful servant, thou knewest that I reap where I sowed not, and gather where I have not strawed:"

Accordingly, the Lord was displeased with his understanding of his actions. Thus saying, you devilish and unthinking servant, for indeed, you knew that I am the creator of all things which gives life in abundance of Love and truths.

KJV Matthew 25: verse 27

Thou oughtest therefore to have put my money to the exchangers, and *then* at my coming I should have received mine own with usury.

Comment appropriately to "Thou oughtest therefore to

have put my money to the exchangers, and *then* at my coming I should have received mine own with usury."

Regardless, it would be best if you had indeed used all my compassion for more wealth with society. Therefore, upon return, you should have presented unto me more wealth and treasures in the heart.

KJV Matthew 25: verse 28

Take therefore the talent from him, and give *it* unto him which hath ten talents.

Comment appropriately to "Take therefore the talent from him, and give *it* unto him which hath ten talents."

To this end, remove what little compassion you held in consciousness; thus, give it unto the soul ten times the value of understanding.

KJV Matthew 25: verse 29

For unto every one that hath shall be given, and he shall have abundance: but from him that hath not shall be taken away even that which he hath.

Comment appropriately to "For unto every one that hath shall be given, and he shall have abundance: but from him that hath not shall be taken away even that which he hath."

With this purpose in mind, the soul obtains more peace, joy, happiness, and Love in spirit. He shall receive more abundantly.

However, he that does not do the work given from the Father shall lose that which he has little of, and thy Lord shall give it to another.

KJV Matthew 25: verse 30

And cast ye the unprofitable servant into outer darkness: there shall be weeping and gnashing of teeth.

Comment appropriately to "And cast ye the unprofitable servant into outer darkness: there shall be weeping and gnashing of teeth."

Therefore, thy Lord shall send away the soul with little to no wealth earned into the darkness of consciousness, where there will be sorrow within the spirit and deep mourning.

KJV Matthew 25: verse 31

When the Son of man shall come in his glory, and all the holy angels with him, then shall he sit upon the throne of his glory:

Comment appropriately to "When the Son of man shall come in his glory, and all the holy angels with him, then shall he sit upon the throne of his glory:"

In amazement, in the second coming of our Lord and Savior because in truth. The glory of God shall unleash all righteousness in the kingdom of heaven with the singing of angels with him.

In all his glory shall sit on the right hand of God the Father All-Mighty indeed.

KJV Matthew 25: verse 32

And before him shall be gathered all nations: and he shall separate them one from another, as a shepherd divideth *his* sheep from the goats:

Comment appropriately to "And before him shall be gathered all nations: and he shall separate them one from another, as a shepherd divideth *his* sheep from the goats:"

Above all, the Son of man shall gather all souls in consciousness (all nations); thus, he shall separate as the Good Shepherd the righteous from the unrighteous.

KJV Matthew 25: verse 33

And he shall set the sheep on his right hand, but the goats on the left.

Comment appropriately to "And he shall set the sheep on his right hand, but the goats on the left."

Therefore, he shall set the righteous-sheep in the heart (right) from the unrighteous-goat (left).

KJV Matthew 25: verse 34

Then shall the King say unto them on his right hand, Come, ye blessed of my Father, inherit the kingdom prepared for you from the foundation of the world:

Comment appropriately to "Then shall the King say unto them on his right hand, Come, ye blessed of my Father, inherit the kingdom prepared for you from the foundation of the world:"

To this end, thy Lord God shall say to his obedient followers who sought after righteousness in his teachings of prayer, transcendental meditation, and solitude.

Come unto me, my good and faithful servants to the Father, our Father takes great pleasure and gives unto you the Kingdom of God in which I have prepared for you.

KJV Matthew 25: verse 35

For I was an hungred, and ye gave me meat: I was thirsty, and ye gave me drink: I was a stranger, and ye took me in:

Comment appropriately to "For I was an hungred, and ye gave me meat: I was thirsty, and ye gave me drink: I was a stranger, and ye took me in:"

Accordingly, when I searched for spiritual food (hungered), you gave me knowledge and understanding (meat for the spiritual body). Thus, when I searched for spiritual truths (thirsty), thy Lord God gave me love (drink) which fulfilled me from within as water well overflows.

Even more so when I was with little spiritual awareness (stranger), thy Lord God gave me refuge (took me in) for my spirit.

KJV Matthew 25: verse 36

Naked, and ye clothed me: I was sick, and ye visited me: I was in prison, and ye came unto me.

Comment appropriately to "Naked, and ye clothed me: I was sick, and ye visited me: I was in prison, and ye came unto me."

Consequently, when I was with unrighteous thoughts and guilt (naked), you prayed for me (clothed me); when I was prideful and boasted (sick), you forgave me (visited me).

Lastly, when I lived in a divided mind of adulterous thinking, my Lord God (came unto me).

KJV Matthew 25: verse 37

Then shall the righteous answer him, saying, Lord, when saw we thee an hungred, and fed *thee?* or thirsty, and gave *thee* drink?

Comment appropriately to "Then shall the righteous answer him, saying, Lord, when saw we thee an hungred, and fed *thee?* or thirsty, and gave *thee* drink?"

Of course, the righteous sheep of the Lord said, when you saw us searching for truths in spirit (hungered) you feed me knowledge? Likewise, when you saw us empty of Love (thirsty), I wasn't aware of you giving me righteous thinking from the heart (drink)?

KJV Matthew 25: verse 38

When saw we thee a stranger, and took *thee* in? or naked, and clothed *thee?*

Comment appropriately to "When saw we thee a stranger, and took *thee* in? or naked, and clothed *thee?*"

In addition, when you saw me with little spiritual awareness (stranger), you gave us righteous thinking? Or unrighteous thoughts and guilt (naked), yet you prayed with me (clothed thee)?

KJV Matthew 25: verse 39

Or when saw we thee sick, or in prison, and came unto thee?

Comment appropriately to "Or when saw we thee sick, or in prison, and came unto thee?"

Furthermore, when I was prideful and boasted (sick) living in my adulterous mind (in prison), you forgave me (came unto thee)?

KJV Matthew 25: verse 40

And the King shall answer and say unto them, Verily I say unto you, Inasmuch as ye have done *it* unto one of the least of these my brethren, ye have done *it* unto me.

Comment appropriately to "And the King shall answer and say unto them, Verily I say unto you, Inasmuch as ye have done *it* unto one of the least of these my brethren, ye have done *it* unto mc."

Without delay, thy Lord God (King) answered them saying, for these truths, I tell you concerning how to enter the kingdom of heaven (Verily) if you have done any of these things for your neighbor, brother, or sister (least of these) you have done it unto the all-in oneness.

JV Matthew 25: verse 41

Then shall he say also unto them on the left hand, Depart from me, ye cursed, into everlasting fire, prepared for the devil and his angels:

Comment appropriately to "Then shall he say also unto them on the left hand, Depart from me, ye cursed, into everlasting fire, prepared for the devil and his angels:"

As a result, our Lord shall say unto to the unrighteous (left hand), depart from me into solitude, you remain in little to low vibration of the kingdom in thy sight, remain in a tormented mind as you prepare for a wicked sense and unrighteous thoughts.

KJV Matthew 25: verse 42

For I was an hungred, and ye gave me no meat: I was thirsty, and ye gave me no drink:

Comment appropriately to "For I was an hungred, and ye gave me no meat: I was thirsty, and ye gave me no drink:"

I searched for knowledge and understanding (hungered) in reasoning, and you gave me no spiritual food (no meat): yet, I was searching for spiritual truths (thirsty), and you gave me unrighteous thoughts and lack of love (no drink).

KJV Matthew 25: verse 43

I was a stranger, and ye took me not in: naked, and ye clothed me not: sick, and in prison, and ye visited me not.

Comment appropriately to "I was a stranger, and ye took me not in: naked, and ye clothed me not: sick, and in prison, and ye visited me not."

In addition, when I was with little spiritual awareness (stranger), you gave me no righteous thinking. Or when I had unrighteous thoughts (naked) and guilt (prison), you didn't pray with me (visited me not).

KJV Matthew 25: verse 44

Then shall they also answer him, saying, Lord, when saw we thee an hungred, or athirst, or a stranger, or naked, or sick, or in prison, and did not minister unto thee?

Comment appropriately to "Then shall they also answer him, saying, Lord, when saw we thee an hungred, or athirst, or a stranger, or naked, or sick, or in prison, and did not minister unto thee?"

With this purpose in mind, yeah Lord, when did we see me searching for righteousness (hungered) and searching for truths in thy Lord Jesus (thirst)?

Or with unrighteous thinking (suffering) or guilt (prison)? Hence, we did not comfort thee?

KJV Matthew 25: verse 45

Then shall he answer them, saying, Verily I say unto you, Inasmuch as ye did *it* not to one of the least of these, ye did *it* not to me.

Comment appropriately to "Then shall he answer them,

saying, Verily I say unto you, Inasmuch as ye did *it* not to one of the least of these, ye did *it* not to me."

Indeed, thy Lord God shall answer saying, truthfully, I tell you these things. For this reason, if you did not do any of these things for your brothers, sisters, or neighbors (least of these).

Then indeed, you did not do this for me!

KJV Matthew 25: verse 46

And these shall go away into everlasting punishment: but the righteous into life eternal.

Comment appropriately to "And these shall go away into everlasting punishment: but the righteous into life eternal."

Therefore, I say unto the unrighteous at heart. For long-suffering continues in the inner workings of the subconscious mind until all righteousness leads to eternal abundance (life).

Matthew Chapter 26

KJV Matthew 26: verse 2

Ye know that after two days is *the feast of* the passover, and the Son of man is betrayed to be crucified.

Comment appropriately to "Ye know that after two days is *the feast of* the passover, and the Son of man is betrayed to be crucified."

Consequently, in a blessing dinner festival is prepared for thy Lord God in remembrance of his sacrifice.

However, Judas Iscariot shall also remember him in his betrayal of the divided mind (human mind) of one Jesus chose with Love before the crucifixion.

KJV Matthew 26: verse 10

When Jesus understood *it*, he said unto them, Why trouble ye the woman? for she hath wrought a good work upon me.

Comment appropriately to "Why trouble ye the woman? for she hath wrought a good work upon me."

In other words, why worry concerning these good deeds graced upon our Lord God; thus, she brings honor upon herself.

KJV Matthew 26: verse 11

For ye have the poor always with you; but me ye have not always.

Comment appropriately to "For ye have the poor always with you; but me ye have not always."

For indeed, you shall always have the unrighteous in mind; however, the Son of man shall reveal himself only in the second coming to you.

KJV Matthew 26: verse 12

For in that she hath poured this ointment on my body, she did *it* for my burial.

Comment appropriately to "For in that she hath poured this ointment on my body, she did *it* for my burial."

Indeed, my beloved has prepared thy Lord for his return to the kingdom with the fragrance of sweet essence.

KJV Matthew 26: verse 13

Verily I say unto you, Wheresoever this gospel shall be preached in the whole world, *there* shall also this, that this woman hath done, be told for a memorial of her.

Comment appropriately to "Verily I say unto you,

Wheresoever this gospel shall be preached in the whole world, *there* shall also this, that this woman hath done, be told for a memorial of her."

With this purpose in mind upon entering the kingdom of heaven, whosoever shall rewrite these gospels to this world. Shall indeed include this marvelous deed in which she honors our Lord and Savior Jesus Christ.

In my obedience to our Lord and Savior Jesus Christ, we give recognition to acknowledgement to **Mary Magdalene** for her humbling heart to our Savior, the Christ, our Messiah. In Jesus' name, we pray, Amen.

KJV Matthew 26: verse 18

And he said, Go into the city to such a man, and say unto him, The Master saith, My time is at hand; I will keep the passover at thy house with my disciples.

Comment appropriately to "Go into the city to such a man, and say unto him, The Master saith, My time is at hand; I will keep the passover at thy house with my disciples."

Therefore, go unto the presence (city) of my servant, for he is aware what his Lord (Master saith) requires in the heart (hand). For this purpose, in thy soul, he will present his followers (disciples) our last supper (Passover).

KJV Matthew 26: verse 21

And as they did eat, he said, Verily I say unto you, that one of you shall betray me.

Comment appropriately to "Verily I say unto you, that one of you shall betray me."

Accept these truths upon entering the kingdom; for indeed, there will be a soul who will betray thy Lord God.

KJV Matthew 26: verse 23

And he answered and said, He that dippeth *his* hand with me in the dish, the same shall betray me.

Comment appropriately to "He that dippeth *his* hand with me in the dish, the same shall betray me."

Moreover, my unrighteous servant shall continue with a broken heart (hand) because of his unrighteousness in thought (betrayal).

KJV Matthew 26: verse 24

The Son of man goeth as it is written of him: but woe unto that man by whom the Son of man is betrayed! it had been good for that man if he had not been born.

Comment appropriately to "The Son of man goeth as it is written of him: but woe unto that man by whom the Son of man is betrayed! it had been good for that man if he had not been born."

However, so shall it be written of our Lord God's betrayal, for with Judas shall indeed live-in long-suffering of this actions.

KJV Matthew 26: verse 25

Then Judas, which betrayed him, answered and said, Master, is it I? He said unto him, Thou hast said.

Comment appropriately to "Thou hast said"

Indeed, by thou word, we are redeemed, and by thy word, we are justified. However, in this case, our Lord is bringing truths from Judas' heart.

KJV Matthew 26: verse 26

And as they were eating, Jesus took bread, and blessed *it*, and brake *it*, and gave *i*t to the disciples, and said, Take, eat; this is my body.

Comment appropriately to "Take, eat; this is my body."

Accept (take), for this is the spiritual food of desires (eat) of my body (spiritual body of Christ).

KJV Matthew 26: verse 27

And he took the cup, and gave thanks, and gave *it* to them, saying, Drink ye all of it;

Comment appropriately to "Drink ye all of it;"

In this manner, take this cup and drink it all because it represents the covenant.

KJV Matthew 26: verse 28

For this is my blood of the New Testament, which is shed for many for the remission of sins.

Comment appropriately to "For this is my blood of the New Testament, which is shed for many for the remission of sins."

Likewise, this is my spiritual life (blood), resurrection, purification concerning my New Commandments. In my Love is for all who genuinely give repentance of their sin in their heart.

KJV Matthew 26: verse 29

But I say unto you, I will not drink henceforth of this fruit of the vine, until that day when I drink it new with you in my Father's kingdom.

Comment appropriately to "But I say unto you, I will not drink henceforth of this fruit of the vine, until that day when I drink it new with you in my Father's kingdom."

Jesus said to his disciples; he shall not take (drink) from the subconscious mind that provides knowledge and understanding until the day I come in the second coming in my Father's kingdom.

KJV Matthew 26: verse 31

Then saith Jesus unto them, All ye shall be offended because of me this night: for it is written, I will smite the shepherd, and the sheep of the flock shall be scattered abroad.

Comment appropriately to "All ye shall be offended because of me this night: for it is written, I will smite the shepherd, and the sheep of the flock shall be scattered abroad."

Indeed, all disciples shall be ashamed in this event. Thus, thy Lord shall receive unjust treatment, and his disciples will not bear witness to these insults.

KJV Matthew 26: verse 32

But after I am risen again, I will go before you into Galilee.

Comment appropriately to "But after I am risen again, I will go before you into Galilee."

After these events, I shall indeed redeem myself and go before you to Galilee.

KJV Matthew 26: verse 34

Jesus said unto him, Verily I say unto thee, That this night, before the cock crow, thou shalt deny me thrice.

Comment appropriately to "Verily I say unto thee,"

For this is the truth concerning how to enter the kingdom of heaven.

Comment appropriately to "That this night, before the cock crow, thou shalt deny me thrice."

Indeed, in a soul's darkness (night) of the conscious Self be unrighteous, then his thoughts in his emotions shall deny the Father, Son, and the Holy Spirit (thrice - three).

KJV Matthew 26: verse 36

Then cometh Jesus with them unto a place called Gethsemane, and saith unto the disciples, Sit ye here, while I go and pray yonder.

Comment appropriately to "Sit ye here, while I go and pray yonder."

Furthermore, be still mindful of your thoughts in your awareness while I watch over you in prayer.

KJV Matthew 26: verse 38

Then saith he unto them, My soul is exceeding sorrowful, even unto death: tarry ye here, and watch with me.

Comment appropriately to "My soul is exceeding sorrowful, even unto death: tarry ye here, and watch with me."

Indeed, my spiritual body is hugely distressed by my sheep, even to the end of the day. Be still right now (tarry ye here) in this moment; visualize our joy with me (watch with me) in solitude.

KJV Matthew 26: verse 39

And he went a little further, and fell on his face, and prayed, saying, O my Father, if it be possible, let this cup pass from me: nevertheless not as I will, but as thou *wilt*.

Comment appropriately to "O my Father, if it be possible, let this cup pass from me: nevertheless not as I will, but as thou *wilt*."

Father, all things are possible in thy kingdom; let this testimony (cup) of your Love be in thy honor. Notwithstanding, not as my (the Son) will, but greater than all will in the kingdom of heaven.

KJV Matthew 26: verse 40

And he cometh unto the disciples, and findeth them asleep, and saith unto Peter, What, could ye not watch with me one hour?

Comment appropriately to "What, could ye not watch with me one hour?"

In short, why are you not able to focus on deep thought for a little while?

KJV Matthew 26: verse 41

Watch and pray, that ye enter not into temptation: the spirit indeed is willing, but the flesh *is* weak.

Comment appropriately to "Watch and pray, that ye enter not into temptation: the spirit indeed is willing, but the flesh *is* weak."

Therefore, be mindful of your thoughts and ask for guidance in righteous thinking that you shall not enter adulterous ways. So, it is effortless to do because the spirit is aware of itself in consciousness.

However, the flesh is indeed a devil of unrighteous ways (flesh is weak).

KJV Matthew 26: verse 42

He went away again the second time, and prayed, saying, O my Father, if this cup may not pass away from me, except I drink it, thy will be done.

Comment appropriately to "O my Father, if this cup may not pass away from me, except I drink it, thy will be done."

Father, for thy testimony (cup), has been given to me in all righteousness. For this reason, you have given me this appointment (the Messiah may not pass the cup from me).

Let thy will be done to and through me.

Note: Be that it may, each of us has an assignment which means, in essence. You have a specific task that must manifest as your cup.

KJV Matthew 26: verse 45

Then cometh he to his disciples, and saith unto them, Sleep on now, and take *your* rest: behold, the hour is at hand, and the Son of man is betrayed into the hands of sinners.

Comment appropriately to "Sleep on now, and take *your* rest: behold, the hour is at hand, and the Son of man is betrayed into the hands of sinners."

Peacefully, walk in the divided mind (sleep); for now, take comfort in me (rest). Therefore, the present moment in my heart of betrayal of the evildoers.

Love and truth must lift the Messiah's glory in the oneness

of the Father.

KJV Matthew 26: verse 46

Rise, let us be going: behold, he is at hand that doth betray me.

Comment appropriately to "Rise, let us be going: behold, he is at hand that doth betray me."

Consequently, raise thy vibrations and do not delay. Indeed, Judas that troubled my heart (hand) sins (doth) in betrayal stands before me.

KJV Matthew 26: verse 50

And Jesus said unto him, Friend, wherefore art thou come? Then came they, and laid hands on Jesus, and took him.

Comment appropriately to "Friend, wherefore art thou come?"

Honestly, my friend, why have you made these choices in the subconscious mind?

KJV Matthew 26: verse 52

Then said Jesus unto him, Put up again thy sword into his place: for all they that take the sword shall perish with the sword.

Comment appropriately to "Put up again thy sword into his place: for all they that take the sword shall perish with the sword."

Wherefore truth, do not resort to disharmonious places of insults (sword). Indeed, all that live by insulting others shall also die in the subconscious mind by humiliation.

KJV Matthew 26: verse 53

Thinkest thou that I cannot now pray to my Father, and he shall presently give me more than twelve legions of angels?

Comment appropriately to "Thinkest thou that I cannot now pray to my Father, and he shall presently give me more than twelve legions of angels?"

Consequently, even as things may appear in the human eyes, our thought appears unto the Father. Also, he is omnipresent, so, therefore, if it is thy will that I should need servants.

I no way in doubt would be the Messiah obtaining over seventy thousand angels (twelve legions) at his beck and call.

KJV Matthew 26: verse 54

But how then shall the scriptures be fulfilled, that thus it must be?

Comment appropriately to "But how then shall the scriptures be fulfilled, that thus it must be?"

However, in haste, how can the crucifixion be done as written in the book of Isaiah.

KJV Matthew 26: verse 55

In that same hour said Jesus to the multitudes, Are ye come

out as against a thief with swords and staves for to take me? I sat daily with you teaching in the temple, and ye laid no hold on me.

Comment appropriately to "Are ye come out as against a thief with swords and staves for to take me?"

Therefore, you come against me in your divided mind of unrighteous doings listening to a priest (thief) with false doctrine hurling endless insults (swords) and the cross (staves) to bear against me!

Comment appropriately to "I sat daily with you teaching in the temple, and ye laid no hold on me."

Indeed, I await your conscious thought on thy Lord for the teaching in your spiritual Self (temple) as you consciously think nothing in mind (ye laid no hold on me), spiritual body, and soul of the Lord God.

KJV Matthew 26: verse 56

But all this was done, that the scriptures of the prophets might be fulfilled. Then all the disciples forsook him, and fled.

Comment appropriately to "But all this was done, that the scriptures of the prophets might be fulfilled."

Indeed, all these things on my prophets shall endure as the Messiah has done. They shall come against you in the divided mind for my sake.

KJV Matthew 26: verse 64

Jesus saith unto him, Thou hast said: nevertheless I say unto you, Hereafter shall ye see the Son of man sitting on the right hand of power, and coming in the clouds of heaven.

Comment appropriately to "Thou hast said: nevertheless I say unto you, Hereafter shall ye see the Son of man sitting on the right hand of power, and coming in the clouds of heaven."

For it has been said, regardless, soon after the crucifixion. Therefore, the Son of man holds all power of Love and truth within the heart (hand) and spiritual body (clouds) of Christ in full consciousness (heaven) of the Father.

Matthew Chapter 27

KJV Matthew 27: verse 11

And Jesus stood before the governor: and the governor asked him, saying, Art thou the King of the Jews? And Jesus said unto him, Thou sayest.

Comment appropriately to "Thou sayest."

In short, by thy words, ye shall be justified.

KJV Matthew 27: verse 46

And about the ninth hour Jesus cried with a loud voice, saying, Eli, Eli, lama sabachthani? that is to say, My God, my God, why hast thou forsaken me?

Comment appropriately to "Eli, Eli, lama sabachthani?"

With this purpose in mind, our Lord Jesus conveys the feelings emotional or physical anguish, in the Messiah's case, being on the cross.

"My God, my God, why hast Thou forsaken me"

Matthew Chapter 28

KJV Matthew 28: verse 9

And as they went to tell his disciples, behold, Jesus met them, saying, All hail. And they came and held him by the feet, and worshipped him.

Comment appropriately to "All hail"

Praise God, for he has risen.

KJV Matthew 28: verse 10

Then said Jesus unto them, Be not afraid: go tell my brethren that they go into Galilee, and there shall they see me.

Comment appropriately to "Be not afraid: go tell my brethren that they go into Galilee, and there shall they see me."

Glory on high, do not fear me. At once, tell thy brothers that the prophecy thy Lord Jesus has risen the dead in spirit. See and bear witness of his Holiness.

KJV Matthew 28: verse 18

And Jesus came and spake unto them, saying, All power is given unto me in heaven and in earth.

Comment appropriately to "All power is given unto me in heaven and in earth."

In truth, all consciousness of the Father is in me to rule over my domain.

KJV Matthew 28: verse 19

Go ye therefore, and teach all nations, baptizing them in the name of the Father, and of the Son, and of the Holy Ghost:

Comment appropriately to "Go ye therefore, and teach all nations, baptizing them in the name of the Father, and of the Son, and of the Holy Ghost:"

For this reason, go out and teach to all who will listen to these things herein my mysteries. Indeed, baptizing each in the Father's name, and of the Son, and the Holy Spirit.

KJV Matthew 28: verse 20

Teaching them to observe all things whatsoever I have commanded you: and, lo, I am with you alway, *even* unto the end of the world. Amen.

Comment appropriately to "Teaching them to observe all things whatsoever I have commanded you: and, lo, I am with you alway, *even* unto the end of the world."

In addition, with Love in your heart, teaching my sheep to honor the Father (all things), obey my commandments.

Indeed, I, your Lord God Jesus Christ, will never leave you as I am always with you, even at the end of the world.

INDEX

Ashes - Refers to tears. A subtle vibrational alignment of one's soul inwardly attributes to painful or harsh lessons instead of happiness.

Awareness - To feel or to have inner knowing without physical evidence.

Birds - Emotional thoughts or ideas held in the subconscious mind.

Birds of the Air - Refers to a group or individual souls who are searching for spiritual truths.

Blind Leaders - Teachers of the Law of Moses. (Old Testament)

Blood - Refers to spiritual life, resurrection, purification.

Bread - Also known as leaven; Spiritual food of knowledge. (See "Lord").

Bones - Refers to the inner structure of the spiritual body (androgynous) without form. Can be either male or female.

Candle/Stick - A soul walking in the darkness of the light.

Children of God – A collective group of souls who have been anointed by God's Holy Spirit.

Church - Refers to all souls within the kingdom of heaven.

Clothing - Refers to the physical body, also known as *raiment*. (Race, Gender, Sexuality, or Social Class).

Clouds - Refers to righteous thoughts or ideas held in between the conscious and subconscious mind which are pure in nature.

Consciousness - Refers to seeing and understanding truths within the conscious mind.

Cornerstone – Refers to the Christ or one who is authorized to judge all by way of our Heavenly Father.

Council - Refers to the ascended spirit guides with higher knowledge.

Darkness - Refers to spiritual blindness or Ignorance of the true spiritual Self. (See "The Self").

Dominion - The Self's genuine desire for completion.

Earth - Refers to your subconscious mind, your inner world.

Eye - Refers to your spiritual eye or your mind's eye in the spiritual body.

Farmers - Those who are authorized to guide souls with clarity the inner workings of spirit while planting seeds.

Fasting - Refers to taking a break in the mind from this world or **transcendental meditation (TM)**.

Field - Refers to the dry land of the subconscious mind. Capable of growing spiritual food of knowledge.

Fire – Refers to a tormented subconscious mind or (lies held in human-mind). Can be referred also as *hell's fire*.

Fish - Refers to the salvation offered through Christ in the resurrection.

Fishermen – Refers to disciples who attract others to Christ by the *Universal Law of Attraction*.

Five Trees in Paradise which Remain Undisturbed - Refers to consciousness - The Tree of **Life**, Tree of **Knowledge**, Tree of **Wisdom**, Tree of **Love**, and the Tree of **Peace**.

Flesh - Refers to the spiritual body of Christ through the oneness of the Father.

Foot - Refers to the soul's journey.

Footstool - Refers to a commonplace vibrational planet/universe structure for lessons. (Gaia – Mother Earth)

Fowl - Refers to emotional thoughts between the conscious and subconscious mind.

Fruit - Teachings of Jesus Christ and food for the spiritual body.

Fruit Tree – Spiritual Knowledge and Understanding.

Garments – Refers to unrighteous thoughts or guilt held in the subconscious mind. (Also referred to as outer garments or sackcloth)

Gnashing of Teeth - Refers to lament of a soul of its evil deeds portrayed during its incarnation not following spirit.

God - Universal Law of Three. "God the Father, God the Son, God the Holy Spirit." All in one accord consciously.

Small "gods" - refers to souls who are seeking the deep meaning of spiritual truths.

Good Works - Refers to the inner works done within the subconscious mind leading to righteousness of the soul. (See "Mighty Work")

Good Soil - Refers to a subconscious mind ready to accept the spiritual teachings of Jesus Christ. (See "Large Fish").

Grass - Refers to knowledge within the subconscious mind.

Grapevine - Refers to religious teaching outside of Father's instructions given unto Jesus Christ in the New Testaments.

Hand - Refers to the soul's spiritual heart.

Heaven - Refers to the conscious mind.

Herbs - Refers to grass or plants in the field or as good seeds. (See "Field").

He that has ears to hear let him hear - Refers to alerting to the elect to listen and understand truths behind the teachings.

House - Refers to you as the soul.

In Earth - Refers to the subconscious mind.

In Heaven - Refers to the conscious mind of the Self. (See "the Self").

I say unto you - Refers to our Lord replacing Old Testament Laws given unto Moses with his new commandments.

Knowledge - Refers to the flesh of the spiritual body.

Lamb - Refers to the True Self. (Fully awakened).

Large Fish - Souls who are attracted to the Fisherman. Ready to accept the teachings of Jesus Christ. (See Small Fish).

Laws of Moses - Also referred to the First Testament, Old Testament or the old-time.

Left Hand - Refers to the spiritual heart in the spiritual body. The left refers to unrighteousness or spiritually dead side. (Refer to "Right Hand")

Light – Refers to conscious awareness, intuitiveness.

Living - Refers to full consciousness. (See "consciousness").

Lord – Refers to keeper of knowledge; (Bread Keeper).

Meat - Refers to the substance or flesh of the spiritual body.

Mighty Works - Refers to the inner works done within the subconscious mind leading to heart chakras of the soul. (See "Good Works")

Mother - Refers to the conscious mind of the Self. (Heaven) Can also be referred to as the Wife to the Self.

Produce – Refers to moral teachings of "Love and Truth."

Religious Teachers - Teachers of the Law of Moses. (Old Testament). Keepers of artificial rules. (See Blind Leaders).

Repentance - Confession of sins of wrongdoing before God.

Right Hand - Refers to the spiritual heart in the spiritual body. The right refers to righteousness or spiritually awaken. (Refer to "Left Hand")

Rock - Love and Truth to stand against the test of time for all eternity.

Sabbath – Refers to a day of rest from the world.

Sage - Enlightened human being currently incarnated.

Salt - Refers to the substance of the subconscious mind in the filament of emotions.

Satan | Devil - Satan is used as a metaphor to describe and characterize man's mind - hence the alter-ego (human mind). To be or state of mind, thus spiritually dead or not awaken.

Savior of the World - Given Authority by the Father. Lamb of God. (See Lamb)

Seas - Refers to the intense emotions within the subconscious mind.

Seasons - Seasons represents a soul's spiritual journey to fulfillment of desires. They are **Autumn** or **Evening** when knowledge is present. **Winter** or **Night** when darkness is present. **Spring** or **Morning** with beginning growth of the soul. **Summer** or **Day** ripened for harvest in the Self's desire for completion.

Seeds - Refers to ideas planted in the subconscious mind.

Serpent - Unrighteous desire and temptations of pleasure leading to adulterous truths.

Servants - Angels in Heaven.

Sheep - Refers to souls who have accepted Jesus Christ as God in Trinity, Lord, and Savior, and the Messiah.

Small Fish - Souls attracted to the Fisherman yet refuse to receive the "Teachings of Jesus Christ" (see Large Fish).

Sower - A spiritual being planting seeds in a field. (See Seeds or Field definition).

sons of God - Refers to sons who have been anointed by the Holy Spirit and awakened. (Notice the small "s").

Stones - Refers to words of hurtful insults.

Swine - Refers to souls who dwell in their divided mind (human mind), delivering ridicule and provoking others.

Sword - Refers to the purity of truth within the word of God. (See "Word of God")

The All - Refers to spiritual and material substance forms of matter from an eternal, indestructible, infinite energy field.

The Good Man - is our Father in heaven.

The Kingdom of God – Refers to the inner strength of an awakened soul in consciousness.

The Kingdom of Heaven - Refers to the conscious mind of our Heavenly Father shared with all souls.

The Lion - Self-image of a physical being. (Human being)

The Living Jesus - Refers Jesus Christ being fully awakened and anointed by the Holy Spirit. He is the **first begotten son** from those known to be "spiritually dead."

The Man - Refers to the actual image of a spiritual being. (Spiritual being).

The man - Small "*m*" refers to the false Self. (Spiritually dead).

The Sea - The collection of minds searching for the truth.

The Self - God or one who has become fully aware of themselves as a spiritual being. One with the Father.

The Son of Man - Refers to the Son of our Father. (Jesus Christ)

The Son of Men - Refers to the Son of a physical man.

The Wife - Refers to the conscious mind of the Self - Heaven within and conscious mind of the Self. (See Mother). Can also become the bridal chamber to the Husbandman.

Thief - Teachers of the Old/First Testament. One who is spiritually blind, not aware of the teachings of Jesus Christ.

Thorns and thistles - Refers to unrighteous thoughts or knowledge with righteous thoughts manifesting together. An altered state of being.

Treasure - Refers to righteousness in thought extending to the heart centers.

Tooth - Refers to understanding and nourishment for one's spiritual body.

Tree - Refers to the Truth.

Verily, I say unto you - This phrase alerts the elect on truths for entering the Kingdom of God.

Vine - Refers to the thoughts and ideas planted from seed in the subconscious mind leading to righteous growth of fruit. (See Fruit).

Vineyard - Means the word of God.

Wailing - Refer to true repentance before God in Heaven.

Water - Refers to the substance of the mind, which is fluid.

Weeds - Refers to the subconscious mind, which is untruths.

Word of God - Serves as hearing the Self's righteous desire of its Self's will.

Yoke - Refers to righteous thought or thinking in mind.

Workings of the Inner Mind.

Conscious Mind - Refers to where all thoughts and desires take place.

Subconscious Mind - Where all feelings take place and memories are stored.

Human Mind - The human mind lies within the subconscious mind, where all human desires derive from the alter ego. It is the "I" in the "I am" of the altered ego. (See "Darkness").

All Rights Reserved.

While every precaution has been taken in the preparation of this book, the publisher assumes no responsibility for errors or omissions, or for damages resulting from the use of the information contained herein.

JESUS CHRIST MYSTERY TEACHINGS THROUGH PARABLES

First edition. First edit of First edition.

Copyright © 2021 Jesse Williams Jr.

Written by Jesse Williams Jr.

www.ingramcontent.com/pod-product-compliance
Lightning Source LLC
Chambersburg PA
CBHW072142100526
44589CB00015B/2047